T0265808

GLORY, GLORY,
GONE

GLORY, GLORY, GONE

The Story of
Tottenham Hotspur's
Regression, Relegation and Rebirth
in the 1970s

SAMUEL ROOKE

First published by Pitch Publishing, 2023

Pitch Publishing
9 Donnington Park,
85 Birdham Road,
Chichester,
West Sussex,
PO20 7AJ
www.pitchpublishing.co.uk
info@pitchpublishing.co.uk

A CIP catalogue record is available for this book
from the British Library.

ISBN 978 1 80150 420 1

Typesetting and origination by Pitch Publishing
Printed and bound in Great Britain by TJ Books, Padstow

Contents

Introduction

TOTTENHAM HOTSPUR have enjoyed two great periods in their 140-year history. The first ran from 1961 to 1972, the club's true 'golden era' under Bill Nicholson. Those 11 years included the Double win, British football's first European trophy, and three FA Cups in seven years.

The second era ran for roughly a decade from 1981 through to the 1991 FA Cup win. Only four trophies were added but Tottenham undoubtedly returned to the top of British and indeed European football with three FA Cups and another UEFA Cup triumph, marking their resurgence from their worst moments.

In the intervening decade, Tottenham had suffered on and off the pitch. The team endured historic humiliations, remarkable crowd violence – even for the time – and the ultimate insult of relegation from the First Division.

The stories of the Tottenham teams of the 1960s and 1980s have been told before, but – until now – that intervening decade has not. Two legendary teams, linked by a decade which has to a great extent eluded examination.

In nine years, Tottenham would bungle the departure of their greatest manager, replace him with an Arsenal legend, escape relegation with a final-day miracle, and begin to rebuild their team in the image of that Highbury great only to watch him walk out, cross north London, and rejoin the Gunners.

That was just the beginning for a decade which saw Spurs sink to their nadir, before returning to rise to new heights.

It is a truly remarkable period and one which reflects trends across the football world at the time, when the fabulous wealth which now defines the game first began to be piled up.

These years also saw the first arrivals of foreign stars, something that Tottenham were to lead from 1978. This set the stage for modern British football – a league so cosmopolitan for so long that it now barely draws comment.

On the darker side, this same time saw a country wracked by social and economic strife, something against which football in general and Tottenham in particular were not insulated. Crowd violence reached new heights, and authorities responded with draconian policies which would culminate in tragedy.

Sam Rooke
January 2023

Part 1 – De Kuip

1

A changing world

THE WINTER of 1962 and into '63 had been the coldest for Britain in centuries. Only 1683/84 and 1739/40 had seen colder recorded temperatures. In January 1963 the average temperature for the entire month had been -2.1°C, and there was snow on the ground in London for three months.

The fountains in Trafalgar Square froze solid and, with undersoil heating not yet common in England, so too did football.[1]

Spurs managed just one match between mid-January and March – a 3-2 win over Arsenal at Highbury – as the seemingly unending cold weather forced game after game to be postponed.

On 22 March, just two weeks after the first frostless morning of the year, the Beatles released their first album – *Please Please Me* – and changed popular culture forever.

Eight months later, *With the Beatles* would follow. Within 18 months of their emergence on the world stage, the pioneering musical icons would add *A Hard Day's Night* and *Beatles for Sale*.

Bob Dylan, Ray Charles, Aretha Franklin and James Brown each put out a new album in 1963. The Beach Boys released three.

---

1   Everton had become the first club in England to install undersoil heating in 1958, costing the Toffees £16,000 before forcing them to redevelop the drainage systems and other elements of their pitch system.

Doctor Who debuted on British television, while James Bond's second theatrical adventure – *From Russia With Love* – was released.

In an instant, the dour, moribund 1950s were gone and a new, more colourful world emerged.

It was the year of films like *The Great Escape*, *The Birds*, and *The Pink Panther*, the big-budget epic *Cleopatra*, and the hit comedy *Bye Bye Birdie*.

Akira Kurosawa, Ingmar Bergman, Federico Fellini and Alfred Hitchcock all had new movies in theatres simultaneously.

London, always a city of global importance, regained a glamour in this period that had been absent since the 1920s.

The shadow of the Second World War, still visible in bomb-damaged buildings and empty spaces where rubble – long since cleared away – had not yet been replaced, began to finally fade for good in this period.

Carnaby Street became a globally known fashion centre. Mods, Hippies, and other subcultures emerged. By 1966 London was crowned 'The Swinging City' by *Time* magazine.

The nation was changing, and trying to change. The United Kingdom failed in its bid to join the European Economic Community in January. French president Charles de Gaulle vetoed the application.

Harold Wilson rose to become leader of the Labour Party, a role in which he would enact profound change in the years to come.

Tottenham Hotspur both reflected and enhanced that glamour and modernity. They were the big-spending club that had done what no one else had done by winning both the First Division and FA Cup in 1961, becoming the first team since 1897 to claim the 'Double'.

This had been orchestrated by manager Bill Nicholson. Nicholson, a former Tottenham player, had the loftiest of ambitions for his club. The Double win, though glorious, was not sufficient for him.

To the so-called 'Team of the Century', Nicholson had added £99,999 goalscorer extraordinaire Jimmy Greaves from AC Milan. He had broken the British transfer record to do it.

Now Nicholson had his sights set on another groundbreaking achievement – he wanted to win in Europe.

Rotterdam's Feijenoord Stadion was completed in 1936 and began hosting football the following year as a colossal new stadium befitting the already three-times champions of the Netherlands, Feyenoord Rotterdam.

Coal baron Daniël George van Beuningen bought the land for the new ground. Its more commonly used name, De Kuip, translates from Dutch as 'the tub' or 'the bowl', evidently a tribute to its then-modern overhanging design, which was inspired by numerous stadiums across Europe and the United States – notably Arsenal's Highbury.

The stadium was fortunate to survive the Second World War, with Rotterdam being extensively damaged. The port city was flattened as both the Allies and the Germans bombed the area heavily. By the end of the war, only the Medieval Grote of Sint-Laurenskerk remained standing in the centre of the city. The German army reportedly considered tearing De Kuip down to harvest the glass, concrete and steel from which it was made.

After the war, the four great light towers which define De Kuip's silhouette were added.

On 15 May 1963 at De Kuip, Tottenham Hotspur met Atlético Madrid in the final of the UEFA Cup Winners' Cup.

Spurs had finished second in England's First Division that season, admittedly well off the pace of champions Everton, and they were just two years removed from completing the first Double of the 20th century.

Spurs had beaten Rangers 8-4 over two legs in the first round, then smashed Slovan Bratislava 6-2 in the quarter-final and saw off Yugoslavian side OFK Beograd 5-2 to reach the final.

Nicholson's team had lost the European Cup semi-final the previous year to eventual champions Benfica. Tottenham had hammered the Portuguese side in the second leg at White Hart Lane but lost 4-3 on aggregate, with many fans convinced that they'd been cheated by refereeing in both legs. Swiss Daniel Mellet overruled two Tottenham goals in Lisbon, before his Danish colleague Aage Poulsen cancelled another in London.

Nicholson had introduced that season a tweak which still lives on, instructing his kit man to prepare white shorts – instead of the usual blue – for Spurs' European matches.

Alan Mullery – who would captain Tottenham to European glory – remembered the impact that that change had on the players, saying, 'The thing that really stood out, for me as a player, was seeing the kit laid out in the dressing room, with white shorts. As a kid, when European football started, it was dominated by Real Madrid, all in white and us wearing white from top to bottom sent out a statement that we believed we were as good as that Real Madrid side. It was such a brilliant idea for us to play all in white, especially under the floodlights which picked the strip out so strongly. It felt like a different, unique experience, something we all wanted to savour and it did inspire us as a team.'

Before the 1963 final, Nicholson, as he so often did, flew out to Spain to personally scout Atlético, watching them wallop Hércules 4-0.

After his expedition, Nicholson felt he had identified a key weakness. He told wingers Terry Dyson and Cliff Jones, 'This will be your night. Take on the full-backs as often as you can. You can beat them.'

Atlético officials made their own scouting mission to White Hart Lane, watching Spurs dismantle Sheffield United 4-2 in May.

Jimmy Greaves scored his 37th goal of the campaign against the Blades, breaking Tottenham's all-time record for goals in a season. Dyson also scored that day, but Atlético's scouts did not heed the warning.

In the dressing room, right before the final kicked off, Nicholson gave a long and passionate speech about just how good Atlético were. He enthused about their strength, ruthlessness and power.

The energy and positivity drained out of the room as Nicholson went on. When the manager left to give the squad a moment, captain Danny Blanchflower – having felt the players deflating under the strength of Nicholson's speech – stood up and proceeded to lift the mood. He went around the room, pointing out the stars that made up Tottenham's mighty team. There was Jimmy Greaves – perhaps the finest striker in the world; Cliff Jones – a brilliant, goalscoring winger. There was Blanchflower himself, and many more besides.

This group of players were the immortal Double winners of 1961 plus Greaves; they had nothing to fear in Atlético.

Atlético were on a £360-per man bonus to win the final – a significant sum in 1963 – but they were taken apart by Tottenham's wingers as Nicholson had predicted.

Tottenham hammered Atlético 5-1. It was an historic victory, the first European trophy won by a British team, and marked the high watermark for Bill Nicholson's Spurs.

The end would come for Nicholson at the same stadium 11 years later.

Dyson, the man of the match in Rotterdam, was advised to retire immediately afterwards by striker Bobby Smith, who said, 'Terry, son, if I were you I'd retire now. You'll never play another match as good as that for the rest of your life.'

Dave Mackay, an icon in midfield and perhaps Spurs' most important individual player, missed the final with a stomach muscle injury, but inside-forward John White recovered from his own injury to make the starting line-up.

Four thousand Spurs fans had crossed the Channel to see their team's tilt at history, and were rewarded with a crushing victory.

Greaves got the opener, White made it 2-0 before half-time, then Dyson scored a brace either side of Greaves's second. Atlético converted a penalty just after the break but Spurs made history with their victory. More than that, and vitally for Nicholson, they had won it in the right way.

The reticent Yorkshireman was utterly committed to attractive football. Attacking, playing to win and entertaining the fans – the last point something that Nicholson repeatedly reinforced to his players – were his guiding principles.

This was the same man who, after his team beat Leicester City in the 1961 FA Cup Final to seal the historic Double, had told his players that he was disappointed in their performance. Nicholson's first stop after the match had not been to see his own players, but to visit the Leicester dressing room to tell them they had been the better team.

This was not a pantomime, some strategy to squeeze even more out of his squad. These were Nicholson's honest convictions. With that in mind, the nature of Spurs' win over Atlético – speed, movement, intelligence and goals – was of at least equal importance in his mind as actually winning the trophy. He was happy enough to make history, but delighted to do so playing his ideal football.

Newspapers the day after the match speculated that, despite his heroics, Dyson might be sold as Nicholson looked to overhaul his team.[2]

It wasn't the first time that Dyson had been considered surplus to requirements. Legendary Liverpool manager Bill Shankly loved to tease the famously dour Nicholson with an anecdote on the subject.

---

2   Dyson kept his place in the team but was sold to Fulham for £5,000 in 1965.

While Shankly was Huddersfield manager, Nicholson tried to sign Denis Law. The forward, who would go on to become an icon of Manchester United and the Scottish national team, was not yet 20 and Huddersfield were playing in the Second Division, but Nicholson had identified him as the attacking spark his team required.

He called Shankly to ask for Law, and offered Dyson in part-exchange. Dyson was still playing in the reserves at the time and Shankly wanted a first-team player to make the deal. Shankly also had concerns about the diminutive Dyson's ability to survive the physical side of the game.

As the conversation went on, Shankly remembered Nicholson getting more and more effusive in his praise of Dyson's toughness, heart and ability.

Ultimately, Shankly wouldn't budge and the deal fell through. Law went to Manchester City instead, eventually joining United two years later – via a season in Italy with Torino – and won the 1968 European Cup and the 1964 Ballon d'Or while with the Old Trafford club.

Dyson stayed at Spurs and was vital in the Double win, being named man of the match at Wembley as they beat Leicester to lift the FA Cup, as well as starring two years later in Rotterdam.

Nicholson, as ever consumed by the next challenge, said after the remarkable victory over Atlético that the defeat to Everton the previous midweek played more on his mind, and that improvements would have to be made to his ageing squad.

That first great team had reached its peak in Rotterdam. Injury, time, and tragedy would compel Nicholson to build another.

2

New rules of the game

TOTTENHAM HAD built their history-making team by making eager use of the transfer market. Bill Nicholson spent, and spent big, to put together a group of players capable of the glories that they had achieved. Spurs, like every other successful side of the era, were taking advantage of a system rigged heavily in their favour. Players were highly restricted by the regulations around contracts and transfers, but that was about to change.

Two huge steps would be taken in as many years. The full consequences of these reforms would not be apparent for some time, but they would swiftly erode Tottenham's position atop English football.

To understand why the changes came when they did, it is necessary to go much further back than the 1960s.

In fact, it was Liverpool's first league title – won in 1900/01 – that was the catalyst for the creation of the repressive, unequal system.

After the championship was won, it came to light that Liverpool's players received an average wage of £7 per week. This was considered an outrage at a time when the average wage was just over £42 per year (less than a pound a week) and fully one-third of Britons were estimated to be living in poverty. Prices were rising, wages falling, and society was far from ready to accept mere footballers being on such good money.

In response to the controversy, the FA decided to institute a cap on wages. Of course this did nothing for those living in poverty, nor even for those who could afford to spend their wages on football. The limit was initially set at £4 per week.

In addition to this restriction, the Football League also instituted a system to regulate the trading of players known as 'retain and transfer'.

The system was complex, but essentially a club owned a player's registration and could refuse to release it if so inclined. This meant that even after their contract had expired a player would not be able to join a new club without their old club's permission.

This was evidently a huge advantage in contract negotiations for the clubs, giving the players absolutely no leverage short of leaving the game entirely.

In 1910 the Southern League, then still a viable competitor with the First Division and up until then playing outside its regulations, agreed to enforce the system. Players no longer had anywhere else to go, bringing the transfer system fully under control.

The sole remaining alternative for players was to seek a contract with clubs outside of FIFA's governance.

The number of leagues both outside this control and able to pay competitive wages was very small.

Manchester United forward Charlie Mitten would infamously challenge the system by moving to Colombian club Independiente Santa Fe in 1950, earning £40 per week with a signing-on bonus of £5,000. Mitten became known as the 'Bogotá Bandit' for this move.

Several of his Manchester United team-mates followed him there but they were the exception.

All were harshly treated upon their return to English football. Mitten himself was fined six months' wages and banned from playing for the same length of time, before eventually being dumped by Manchester United at Fulham.

In 1959, Newcastle player George Eastham refused to sign a new contract and asked for a transfer. His club refused the request and simply held his registration. After Eastham sat out for a year, Newcastle agreed a transfer with Arsenal but the player refused to go. Instead he took Newcastle to court, suing on the basis of a restraint of trade. Eastham won his case and the 'retain' aspect of the system was dismantled. It was a huge victory for players and would echo throughout English football as players could now have some direct influence over their futures.

Players wouldn't be truly free in terms of their control of their careers until the Bosman ruling in 1995 which facilitated genuine 'free' transfers.

In 1960 the Professional Footballers' Association (PFA) decided to challenge the wage cap. Weekly salaries were limited to £20 per week during the season and £17 per week during the summer. This gave players an annual wage below that of a degree-qualified teacher or an army platoon sergeant.

It must be mentioned that salaries were broadly more equitable in the 1960s. A fully qualified NHS doctor earned around £2,000 per year (roughly £40 per week). An MP's salary in the early 1960s was just £1,000, although they were allowed £750 per year for expenses.

The advent of television and the growth of the British economy generally – GDP had quadrupled since 1941 – meant that the game was awash with money, but the players were still not seeing their fair share.

In April 1960 the PFA made four official demands: the abolition of the maximum wage, the right of players to a share of transfer fees, the creation of a new transfer system, and the creation of new contracts.

Blackburn Rovers chairman Jim Wilkinson argued that even a £30 maximum should be opposed as 'it would be suicide for many clubs'.

Alan Hardaker, the secretary of the Football League, insisted that both the retain and transfer system and the maximum wage were necessary for the survival of English football. He wrote that the 'chaotic conditions that existed before the League was formed' were proof of that necessity. The fact that he was referring to 1888 – more than 70 years earlier and a hugely different world – seemed not to influence his thinking.

Another factor that the authorities failed to consider was public opinion, which had shifted markedly since 1901 and was now firmly on the side of the players.

In January 1961 the players' union threatened to go on strike, although the authorities folded three days before the action was due to start. The maximum wage was abolished, testimonials were made an official part of players' contracts (due after eight years of service) and a minimum wage for retained players was instituted. The final point meant that clubs could still hold out-of-contract players' registration against their will, but at least they would be compelled to pay them, which had not previously been the case.

Jimmy Hill, chairman of the PFA, announced 'a historic moment for football in this country' as Fulham star Johnny Haynes soon became the first player to earn £100 per week.

As it turned out, clubs did not collapse.

These reforms had an instant impact on the transfer market and on the balance of power in European football. The world transfer record, which had steadily ticked up since the sale of Willie Groves from West Bromwich Albion to Aston Villa in 1893 for £100, increased tenfold in the decade after these decisions.

But British clubs disappear from the list.

For the first 60 years of professional football, the world record had been held almost exclusively by British clubs. Argentinian team River Plate had been the sole exception, breaking the record to sign Bernabé Ferreyra in 1932. That outlier also came during the Great Depression, which struck Argentina comparatively lightly. While major European nations, plus the United States, Australia and many others reeled under unemployment rates in excess of 30 per cent, Argentina's only rose to around ten per cent and had returned to normal by 1935.

Italian football took over in the 1950s and only two English clubs – Newcastle for Alan Shearer in 1996 and Manchester United for Paul Pogba 20 years later – have subsequently held the world record.

With player power increasing in the wake of the two reforms to the English transfer system, the nature of the market changed fundamentally and instead of competing with transfer fees, clubs weaponised wages.

At first, the lifting of the wage cap worked in Tottenham's favour. The signing of Jimmy Greaves, earning £7,000 per year in Italy with AC Milan, was only possible because Spurs could suddenly offer comparable wages.

However, despite having built the great Double team via the enthusiastic use of their chequebook, there was a reluctance at the club to be so free with wages.

In 1963 Bill Nicholson missed out on the signature of a player he wanted for the first time as Tottenham coach. Alex Scott, the Scotland winger, had chosen Everton instead of Spurs in February when he moved from Rangers. Scott would prove vital as his new club beat Tottenham to the title that season.

Spurs finished second and Scott shone in a decisive 1-0 win at Goodison Park in April.

Scott had cost Everton £46,000 and his arrival took the Toffees' total spending to £340,000. This sum was even more than Tottenham had spent to construct their Double team.

Spurs' spending in the late 1950s and early 1960s had attracted much comment, but things were now accelerating to another level.

With wages surging, ticket prices followed. At Manchester United, standing tickets jumped from 12.5p in 1960/61 to £1.20 by the end of the 1970s, an average annual price rise of around 40 per cent.

There was a consolidation of power in English football among the biggest clubs. In the 17 years from the resumption of football after the end of the war until 1963, ten different teams won the First Division title. In the same period there were 13 different winners of the FA Cup.

It would take until 1995, when Blackburn won the new Premier League – themselves benefitting from significant owner spending – for the same number of different clubs to win the top title.

Coventry's shock FA Cup win over Tottenham in 1987 made them the 13th different club to win the competition since the end of retain and transfer.

The diminution of variety among champions served to reinforce the advantage enjoyed by those clubs. Victory in the 1970s was simply worth more in monetary terms than it had been in previous decades.

3

The end of the Double team

EVERY GREAT team must eventually be broken up. Time is the trap which closes around even the greatest champions. That process can be managed, and Bill Nicholson's Tottenham certainly tried, but the break-up of the Double team was accelerated first by misfortune, then by genuine tragedy.

The *Football Post* speculated in August 1963 that the end of the great team could be near.

Welsh winger Terry Medwin became the first of the Double winners to leave Spurs. Only 31, Medwin fractured his leg playing in a friendly match against a National Football League XI in Cape Town. Rather than stay with the team for the rest of their tour of South Africa, Medwin flew straight home, telling reporters that he didn't want his wife to worry.

Medwin hoped to return in October, then January, then March. In July, the company processing his playing insurance sent a doctor to determine whether he would ever return. Medwin did not give up the fight to return to playing for Tottenham until January of 1965. For 18 months, the Welshman worked on his fitness, refusing to relinquish his hopes, but finally conceded that he would not be able to return.

In December 1963, five months after Medwin's injury, Dave Mackay suffered a hideous leg break of his own. Mackay, the heart of the Double team, would be kept out of action for nine months. Unlike Medwin, Mackay would return, but Tottenham were robbed of a defining player just as many of his team-mates began to feel their age.

Despite the absence of Mackay, Spurs finished fourth in 1963/64. Jimmy Greaves was the top scorer in the division for the second consecutive season, scoring 36 times.

Their defence of the Cup Winners' Cup faltered at the first hurdle as a late second-leg brace from Bobby Charlton took Manchester United through at Spurs' expense in the second round.

The Double team was creaking. Twice that season Spurs went to Lancashire and were hammered, both times by a 7-2 scoreline. The first occurred in September against Blackburn. Ten of Spurs' starting 11 had been in the 1961 glory side, with Greaves being the only addition. The second, near the end of the season at Turf Moor against Burnley, was the final appearance for Bobby Smith. Mel Hopkins had made his own final bow a few weeks earlier.

In April, captain and playmaker Danny Blanchflower – the man considered to be Nicholson's brains on the pitch and the poetic soul of the team – retired. Despite his desire to emulate his hero Stanley Matthews – who set the record as the oldest player in English top flight history when he made his final appearance for Stoke City at 50 years and five days – Blanchflower succumbed to a knee injury and ended his career at the relatively tender age of 38.

Blanchflower hadn't played for the first team since the previous November, when on a famously foggy night he had struggled to contain Denis Law – who scored a hat-trick – and Tottenham were hammered 4-1.

The Northern Irishman had joined Tottenham for a significant fee as a 29-year-old from Aston Villa, signed by championship-winning manager Arthur Rowe. He actually took future manager Nicholson's place in the team.

Arsenal had wanted to sign Blanchflower, but refused to spend the record £30,000 fee demanded by Villa.

Initially Blanchflower had had some issues, particularly with Nicholson's predecessor Jimmy Anderson. Anderson had dropped him shortly after taking charge.

When Nicholson was first appointed, he too dropped the midfield conductor. Reflecting on the poor run which had cost his predecessor his job, Nicholson admitted, 'Danny was a culprit in that bad run, taking too many liberties. He was an expensive luxury in a poor side.'

The two clashed on this point throughout Nicholson's first months as manager. Their relationship deteriorated at one stage, to the extent that Blanchflower suggested he be transferred elsewhere.

He was dropped temporarily, but was restored to the starting line-up as results fell away. Nicholson argued afterwards, 'After my prodding on the point, he became a better defensive player. When a move broke down, he had to be a defender along with the others.'

Celtic legend Bertie Peacock, Blanchflower's international team-mate for Northern Ireland, disputed that the Spurs man was ever a 'luxury'. Peacock said, 'He could defend – he was essentially an attacker with tremendous vision, but he wanted to be successful so he knew the value of a strong defence. He was essentially a flair player, but he could tackle too.'

But Nicholson and Blanchflower believed that winning wasn't enough – you had to do it with style. Blanchflower would say, 'Football is not entirely about winning ... it's about glory, performing in style, having a bit of flourish in everything you do.'

Blanchflower was the footballing love of Nicholson's life, though he would have never put it in such terms. His vision, his reading of the game and his arrogance with the ball at his feet made him the most influential player of that period. White was to play the same role in Nicholson's second act.

As Spurs won the Double, Blanchflower was named Football Writers' Association (FWA) Footballer of the Year.

It was the second time he'd won it, the first coming the year before Nicholson was appointed.

Blanchflower was the captain of the Double team and a true leader. In the summer of 1961 Nicholson offered to raise his annual salary to £4,000, with the rest of the squad to be paid £3,500. Blanchflower told him it was unacceptable, instead asking £3,500 for himself and £4,000 each for his team-mates. He wanted the players to know that he had gotten them the best deal possible.

On the pitch, there were few who could match Blanchflower's skill and perhaps none with his vehement commitment to positive, attacking football. Cliff Jones insisted that Nicholson was the boss off the pitch, but Blanchflower was the manager on it.

How, therefore, could Tottenham replace such an influential player? There was a succession plan in the shape of John White – 'the Ghost of White Hart Lane'.[3]

Nicholson had planned to build his new team around the genius of White, having told him that he would replace the ageing Blanchflower as the brains of the side.

Blanchflower had actually recommended the signing of White, after facing him for Northern Ireland against Scotland. White's Scotland team-mate Dave Mackay concurred, telling his manager, 'He's great. One of the best I've ever seen for finding the open spaces. If we've a chance of signing him we'll not go wrong,' and Nicholson made the move.

White joined Tottenham from Falkirk in 1959 for £20,000. When he signed, the fee made headlines as it took the combined spending on Spurs' squad to a 'staggering' £250,000.

His debut was delayed due to his selection in the Scottish League representative team, meaning that he missed Tottenham's top-of-the-table match against Wolverhampton

---

3   It should be noted that his nickname refers to his otherworldly sense of timing and ability to appear unmarked in the box.

Wanderers. Wolves manager Stan Cullis had been trying to sign White too, before Nicholson clinched the deal.

Spurs didn't miss him however, hammering Wolves 5-1 at White Hart Lane in front of 59,344 fans. Bobby Smith scored four goals and Jones added the fifth.

Among the crowd that day was American actress Jayne Mansfield, an invited guest of the Tottenham directors. At the time, Mansfield was thought to be the most written-about person in the world. Mansfield posed on the edge of the directors' box to take a famous photo, featuring thousands of adoring fans.

White scored on his debut the following week but Spurs lost to Sheffield Wednesday, although with his addition they had an excellent team. They finished just three points off the top that season, and the stage was set for the historic 1960/61 campaign.

White was a magnificent Scottish forward, somewhat underrated by history but not by anyone who played alongside – or against – him. Nicholson eventually found his best position to be at inside-right.

During his time at the club, Spurs won just once when White was unavailable, a testament to his value to one of football's greatest sides.

White was killed after being struck by lightning on 21 July 1964, on the ninth hole of Crews Hill golf course in Enfield, just a few miles from Tottenham's training ground. His death was a cruel blow, a tragedy that marked a generation of football fans. Journalist John Crace called it 'football's JFK moment'.

His son, Rob White, wrote movingly about his father and described John as 'not a component but a complete original, unrepeatable, irreplaceable'.

Spurs had actually taken their team photo for the 1964/65 season the same morning, with the smiling White included. It was retaken ten days later, short of one club legend.

4

Nicholson's next great team

THE INJURY to Dave Mackay and the imminent retirement of Danny Blanchflower had essentially deprived Tottenham's great team of its heart and soul, respectively.

Injuries and age are one thing, predictable and expected parts of a physical game, but the death of John White was quite another. White would have been at the forefront of Tottenham's future but now that future would take on a different form altogether.

In August 1964, Mackay had written in his *Daily Mirror* column, 'Fans didn't realise that success like ours couldn't last. It never has with any club and never will.'

Having put together his Double-winning team in little more than a year, Bill Nicholson tried to repeat the trick in 1963/64.

Despite the drastic changes, Spurs were four points clear at the top of the First Division at the end of February 1964. Following a 3-1 victory over Arsenal, newspapers were keen to crown them champions.

In March, Alan Mullery joined from Fulham having been initially reluctant to leave. Having read that Spurs were also likely to sign West Ham United's Bobby Moore, Mullery was worried that Nicholson would play him as a full-back.

Mullery was eventually convinced but struggled initially to find his place at Tottenham. In fact, Nicholson delayed the deal by a day, insisting that Mullery play one more match for the Cottagers – against Spurs' title rivals Liverpool – and he duly did so, starring in an upset win.

Tottenham's supporters were convinced that Mullery should be a direct replacement for Blanchflower or Mackay, but his own style was something quite different and he suffered for it.

Mullery joined Spurs as an England under-23 player, and was expected to swiftly move into the senior team. With a home World Cup just two years away, a place in the England team assumed ever greater value. The first England squad selected after Mullery's move to Spurs caused much comment, though, when he was only named as a reserve. Mullery would not be selected for the 1966 World Cup and Spurs were only represented in the finals by Jimmy Greaves.

In the same month, winger Jimmy Robertson swapped St Mirren Park for White Hart Lane in a £25,000 deal. Robertson was an amateur for Cowdenbeath in 1962. He signed for Spurs as a Scotland international just two years later, completing a remarkable rise.

Nicholson also gambled on the signing of Arsenal centre-half Laurie Brown. Brown had played as a forward in amateur football, and Nicholson planned on restoring him to that role after paying £40,000 for him.

The 1963/64 season had echoes of 1959/60 for Tottenham. They had mounted a serious title challenge, but were still in the process of building their team.

Despite the additions of Mullery, Brown and Robertson, Greaves and Jones began to struggle with injury and Spurs' form collapsed. Having been four points clear of second-placed Blackburn with a game in hand they ultimately finished fourth. They lost four of five matches in March, collecting just a single point in a draw with Fulham.

At the same time, Liverpool won eight out of nine to surge to the top of the table. Liverpool and Tottenham played each other twice in three days that month, with the Reds winning both matches 3-1 as they went on to take the title by six points.

With Bill Brown now 33, Nicholson's next concern was a new goalkeeper after his backup John Hollowbread had been sold to Southampton. Hollowbread had only made 67 appearances for Spurs, but had been at the club since Nicholson's days as a player.

Having been so successful in the Scottish market previously, Nicholson looked there again and discovered 19-year-old Bobby Clark of Queen's Park. Nicholson made a 'good offer', according to Clark, but the young Scot decided to turn down the move. A year later he would join Aberdeen where he became a club legend and Scotland's number one.

Having failed to sign Clark, Nicholson looked closer to home and moved for Watford's Pat Jennings. A prodigy, Jennings had been playing under-19 football at the age of 11 in Northern Ireland. He had come to prominence playing in the European Youth Championships, played in England, where he led Northern Ireland to the final at Wembley. They lost to England but Jennings was soon back, making the move to Vicarage Road in May 1963 from Newry Town for £6,500.

Not expecting to play much in his first season, Jennings did actually make several appearances because of that especially snowy winter which pushed the football calendar back.

Incumbent keeper Dave Underwood gave up his place for the final two matches of the season and so Jennings, still a month short of his 18th birthday, made his Football League debut. That first match of the 1,105 he would play in club and international football was a 2-2 draw against QPR.

Underwood, who was double Jennings's age and had been at the club for four years, never played again.[4] Instead, Jennings made 52 consecutive appearances.

---

4   Underwood was credited with helping Tottenham legend Jimmy Greaves deal with alcoholism while chairman of Barnet a decade later.

Watford needed to win the final game of the following season to be promoted to the Second Division, but they lost 2-1 to Port Vale.

The previous summer, former Nicholson team-mate Ron Burgess – a key part of the First Division-winning Tottenham side known as the 'push and run' team – had been appointed as Watford manager.

After just failing to achieve promotion, Burgess and Nicholson got in contact and began to work out a deal. Jennings was initially reluctant to make the leap from the Third Division to Tottenham. Nicholson flew to Ireland to convince him but Jennings, having just joined Watford the previous year and a teenager like Clark, was also unsure about making the move.

Knowing that it was typical for such a transfer, he asked Watford for a bonus. Burgess refused, but Nicholson agreed to pay him £100 out of his own pocket.

Jennings asked for time to think it over and flew back to Northern Ireland. Upon his return, he received a letter written by Nicholson, urging him to accept his offer and join Tottenham. The giant 18-year-old agreed to join, and swiftly became a legend.

The next season Spurs were cursed with inconsistency. They scored seven goals against Wolves, six against Leicester and five against Blackburn Rovers, but also lost 4-1 three times over the season. With just one goalless draw in the entire campaign, Tottenham were nothing if not entertaining.

After enduring his first few months at Spurs, Alan Mullery knocked Chelsea winger Bert Murray over the advertising hoardings in a 1-1 draw in October. Most of the 52,927 people at White Hart Lane roared and suddenly Mullery had found himself.

A few days later he was in a car accident and his wife June went through the windscreen. She survived but received 200 stitches in her face. Mullery had cracked ribs and told

Nicholson that there was no way he could play in Spurs' next match. Nicholson insisted, but Mullery told him, 'I could die.' His manager responded, 'We'll give you a good funeral.' Mullery played and set up two goals as Spurs won 5-1.

In December, Scotland striker Alan Gilzean was added for £72,500[5] from Dundee. Spurs were forced to raise their offer when Sunderland got involved in the bidding.

The following January, promising full-back Joe Kinnear signed professional forms with Spurs, leaving St Albans City where he had been playing as an amateur. Then in May, Bill Nicholson signed Cyril Knowles from Middlesbrough for £45,000.

Liverpool ran away with the league but Spurs were in the battle for second place until February. A tight 1-0 defeat at Anfield, followed by a 5-5 draw at home to Villa, sparked another late-season collapse.

With Greaves sidelined for three months due to hepatitis they lost seven of their last 12 league matches to finish eighth.

Within eight months, Nicholson had put together his second great team. Jennings, Mullery, Gilzean and Knowles would be virtually ever-present for years to come while Robertson would also play his part in a trophy-laden period for the club.

On a less positive note, Dave Mackay had broken his leg once more. While his toughness was never questioned, Nicholson began to doubt whether the Scot could ever truly reach his best form again.

---

5   To contextualise Spurs' spending, the world transfer record at the time was £250,000, which Roma had spent on Italy striker Angelo Sormani the previous year. Sormani lasted just one season in Rome.

5

A finishing touch

IN JULY 1966, taking advantage of a contract dispute, Bill Nicholson added the great Welsh centre-back Mike England from Blackburn Rovers. It was said in the press that Alan Gilzean, who had only arrived at White Hart Lane the previous year, would be offered in a swap deal. Then it was reported that Nicholson and Blackburn boss Jack Marshall had both been on a holiday in the Yorkshire resort town of Scarborough.

In August, with the deal still not done, Stoke City offered £100,000, and Manchester United were also trying to get England signed up. By mid-August United had dropped out, unable to afford the asking price. Nicholson, speaking to journalists during a pre-season tournament in Spain, admitted that he was 'very interested' in acquiring the defender. Stoke announced record profits, and briefed reporters that the difference between their offer and Blackburn's asking price for England would soon be overcome.

On 19 August the deal was finally confirmed – England had signed for Tottenham. In the end, Spurs had offered £95,000, less than the club record fee they had paid for Jimmy Greaves in 1961.[6]

---

6 England's transfer, and that of Alan Ball to Everton for £110,000, raised complaints in the press. With a national income freeze put in place by the Labour government, the wages of ordinary people were fixed for the next six months. The sight of footballers taking rich new contracts did not feel like the solidarity being preached from Westminster.

Tottenham's manager was reportedly involved in 'secret negotiations' to sign England World Cup winner Bobby Moore from West Ham, but that deal never got over the line. Nicholson's disappointment at never getting his hands on Moore would become a legendary and eternal 'what if' for Spurs and their fans.

England made his debut against Leeds United on 20 August, a 3-1 win in which he started nervously but soon found his feet. This was the match in which the infamous photo of Dave Mackay grabbing Billy Bremner by the shirt was taken.[7] It had taken him a little longer the second time, but Nicholson had once again rapidly laid the foundations of a great team. This group of players would collect six trophies and put together two title chases.

In 1967 Spurs went on a remarkable run after the turn of the year, going 16 games unbeaten in the league and reaching the FA Cup Final – their third under Nicholson.

This came after they had travelled to Old Trafford in January to face a rampant Manchester United side. Victory for Spurs would have taken them level at the top with the Red Devils, while defeat would have opened up a significant gap.

Gilzean, who had injured his thigh scoring in a win against Arsenal the previous weekend, was unavailable and Frank Saul played in his place. Mackay was also missing, with Eddie Clayton making a rare appearance.

Jennings was heroic, making a great save in the opening minute. Jimmy Robertson then played 20-year-old midfielder Keith Weller in for a good chance but he shot wide. Weller again went close but George Best and Bobby Charlton were keeping Jennings busy.

While Jennings shone for Spurs, United keeper Alex Stepney made the finest save of all when he denied Greaves from ten yards out in the opening minutes.

---

7   Mackay disliked the famous photo, believing it portrayed him as a bully.

United got the winner when a mix-up between Jennings and England left Best free to pass for Scotland striker David Herd to score.

With 15 minutes to play, Weller had yet another chance but with United's defenders sprawling and Stepney's goal open, he hooked his shot over the bar.

In the dying moments England headed a Greaves corner towards goal. The Spurs players appealed for a goal, but the referee waved play on. Not for the last time at Old Trafford, Tottenham were denied a likely goal by a referee's interpretation. Despite the result, the performance was important for Spurs. The *Daily Mirror*'s match report said, 'Tottenham have at last remembered who they are.' *The People* said Spurs could have played 'ten times worse and won'.

The tight 1-0 defeat was Tottenham's final loss of the season. United couldn't be caught though, and finished the season as champions. The four-point swing of that match proved the final margin in the league table.

United took the league, but Spurs had a date with Chelsea in the FA Cup Final – the 'Cockney Cup Final', the first all-London final. The capital was buzzing with anticipation. Ticket touts were reselling tickets valued at £1 for 25 times face value the day before the match, warning punters that the price would double again the following morning.

In October 1966, Tottenham legend Len Duquemin had predicted that Spurs would win the FA Cup and only lose one more match in the entire season. They promptly lost five of their next six, but the second part of his prediction had a good chance of coming true.

Tottenham went into the final filled with experience of the unique challenges of playing at Wembley. Pat Jennings, England, Greaves, Mackay, Cliff Jones and Terry Venables had all won at the national stadium, while Chelsea could boast just two players with that experience: Eddie McCreadie and Bobby Tambling.

Greaves had already scored 201 goals for Spurs and was the club's second-highest goalscorer, seven behind Double-winner Bobby Smith, who had left in 1964. Greaves was also second on Chelsea's all time list, having struck 132 times for the Blues.

Spurs were heavily favoured to win and Chelsea boss Tommy Docherty admitted before the match that he would instruct his players to play conservatively, saying, 'We are not going to Wembley to entertain anyone.'

The Blues had thumped Spurs 3-0 earlier in the season, but that had been before the additions of Venables, Joe Kinnear and Robertson to the starting XI.

A crowd of 100,000 packed Wembley and received a spectacle of utter dominance from Tottenham.

After the coin toss, the two sides switched ends but Jennings failed to notice and continued running through his pre-game rituals at the wrong end of the pitch.

Both clubs fielded the same XIs which had won their respective semi-finals. It was noted in the build-up that the 'aristocrats' of Tottenham fielded a team which had cost over £550,000 to assemble.

Chelsea full-back Allan Harris nearly gifted Spurs an opener when he swung and missed at a clearance in his own box, leaving Frank Saul free but Harris recovered quickly enough to deny Saul, though he was injured in the attempt.

But for spectacular goalkeeping from Chelsea's Peter Bonetti – who won a place in the England team with his performance – Spurs' right-winger Saul could have had two early goals. His first attempt, a curving shot from 20 yards, required a full-length diving save from Bonetti. Moments later Robertson swung in a cross to Saul but he headed over the bar.

Venables tried to lob Bonetti from distance but, with some difficulty, the Chelsea keeper scrambled to save the chance.

Greaves almost opened the scoring with a searing free kick which just cleared the crossbar after Mullery was fouled in the act of shooting. Robertson then took another shot from the edge of the area, this time firing just over as the Tottenham pressure continued to build.

Robertson finally put Spurs into the lead shortly before half-time with a half volley following a deflected Mullery shot, and after the break Jennings made a spectacular one-handed save, reaching behind his back to claw Tony Hateley's shot off the line. Then Mullery forced yet another athletic stop from Bonetti before Greaves fired in a wicked shot from distance that Bonetti again was equal to.

Saul, who had scored in the 6-0 quarter-final hammering of Birmingham and the decisive goal in a tight 2-1 win over Nottingham Forest in the semi-final, added Spurs' second at Wembley too.

Mackay's long throw found Robertson who pushed the ball into Saul's path. Saul stabbed at the chance, beating Bonetti to double the lead, but he admitted afterwards that he hadn't had time to aim and instead shot blindly.

The final finished 2-1 – after Tambling scored a late consolation goal – but such was Spurs' dominance on the day that match reports uniformly record that scoreline as something of an injustice. The victory earned Tottenham a place in the 1967 Charity Shield and the UEFA Cup Winners' Cup.

Spurs fan and London businessman Morris Keston laid on a £1,000 party for the players at the Hilton Hotel that lasted well into the following morning. A few hours later, the players climbed aboard the open-topped bus for the trophy parade.

6

Nicholson's final overhaul

THE 1967/68 season began well enough with the Charity
Shield match against champions Manchester United.
Pat Jennings scored from the edge of his own area in a
thrilling 3-3 draw. The league campaign was something of a
disappointment, though, as Spurs finished sixth.

In September, Spurs were thrashed 4-0 in the north
London derby, failing to score against Arsenal for the first
time in 24 matches – a streak stretching back to 1955.

During the season, Bill Nicholson made significant moves
in the transfer market, rejuvenating and strengthening his
side. The biggest signing was that of striker Martin Chivers,
who joined in January from Southampton for a British record
fee of £125,000.[8]

Nicholson admitted that he hadn't even been looking to
sign a striker. Southampton manager Ted Bates made an ill-
advised attempt to scare off potential suitors for his young star
by naming a price he believed would be unthinkable. This
tactic backfired spectacularly, merely alerting Nicholson to
Chivers' availability. It shocked Chivers, too, who learned
that he was available to be sold from a newspaper headline.

Nicholson admitted to journalists at the time, 'My big
need was for a defender and I had hardly given forwards a

---

8   The deal was broken down as £92,500 in cash plus Frank Saul. The
     previous record had been Manchester United's acquisition of Denis Law
     from Torino for £115,000 in July 1962.

glance. But because you are looking for one type of player it does not mean you can afford to look away when a different player comes on to the market. There are so few available and the chance may not come around again.'

'Big Chiv' would endure a difficult relationship with Nicholson as a player, always feeling that the old Yorkshireman was too tough on him, but the two became close after his playing career ended.

The veteran Jimmy Greaves was also entering his final year at Spurs – even if he didn't yet know it. It had been Greaves who first planted the seed of coming to Tottenham in Chivers' mind, sounding him out on a potential move while the pair were playing for an English League XI against the Irish League.

Greaves put the question directly to Chivers, asking, 'Would you come to Tottenham?' Chivers responded that it was a 'bloody stupid question. Of course I would'.

Following this discussion, Chivers asked Bates and he was told that the only way he would be sold was if he wrote an official transfer request. Knowing of Spurs' interest, Chivers made his request in writing, and Nicholson swiftly moved to close the deal.

Chivers had been signed to play the Bobby Smith role, the strong and physically dominant centre-forward meant to help get the best out of Greaves's final years, but he would instead end up as his replacement.

For better or worse, Chivers was the emblematic player of Nicholson's final period. When he was at his best, Tottenham remained a dominant, trophy-winning team, but when the player's form waned, so too did the team's.

On his debut, Chivers set up Greaves and then scored himself as Spurs broke a 24-year winless run, beating Sheffield Wednesday at Hillsborough for the first time since the war.

Dave Mackay and Cliff Jones, the last of the Double team, moved on that season, too. Mackay dropped down into the Second Division, joining Brian Clough's Derby County. The lionhearted Scot was allowed to leave for just £5,000 and he proved that he was far from finished, leading the Rams to the title and promotion to the First Division for the first time since 1953.

Mackay was jointly named FWA Footballer of the Year alongside Manchester City's Tony Book as he dropped into a sweeping role, turning defence into attack and knitting Clough's team together.

Meanwhile, Jones – a player for whom Juventus had reportedly once offered £100,000 – moved to Second Division side Fulham for £5,000. He followed them down to the third tier the next season as the Cottagers finished bottom of each league in succession. The Welsh winger was not the star he had been at Tottenham for a decade, and injuries curtailed these final years of a glittering career, but he still shone on occasion in west London.

Despite Chivers' addition, the 1968/69 season was little better for Spurs, yielding a seventh-placed finish and a somewhat promising FA Cup run which ended at Maine Road against Manchester City in March.

After a slow start, Chivers found his place alongside the Jimmy Greaves-Alan Gilzean partnership and scored six of Spurs' 15 goals as the team went on a run, winning four in five matches. But disaster struck when Chivers suffered an appalling knee injury in September during a win over Nottingham Forest. He had shattered his knee, an injury so unpleasant that even his team-mates – experienced and hard footballers though they were – were distressed by it. Chivers was carried off and didn't return until the following August. He didn't even kick a football for ten months.

The 1969/70 season was Spurs' worst under Nicholson as they finished 11th and flopped in both cups. Wolves knocked them out in their first appearance in the League Cup, while Crystal Palace beat them in the FA Cup fourth round after a replay on a miserable Wednesday night. In the dressing room after the match, Nicholson told the players that it was the worst day of his career. He said that he was heartbroken and warned the players of an imminent shake-up, summing up simply by saying, 'I am paid to field a team that wins matches, not loses them.'

The following day, a rare day off given to the squad, Greaves ran into Phil Beal at the training ground and told him he'd been dropped, adding, 'I think I've played my last game for Tottenham.' Greaves was right. In the next training session, Nicholson announced to the squad that Greaves, Gilzean, Kinnear, Knowles and Perryman would be omitted for the next game. He clarified that only Perryman was being rested. The rest had been dropped.

After the players had all gone home, Nicholson remained to speak with the press. For him, a line had been crossed:

'This was something that had to be done. We have reached the stage where there was no alternative. Now we must rebuild from the ashes. I accept my share of the responsibility for what has gone wrong. Now the players must realise they have not been doing enough.'

The game after Palace saw a very young team beaten 1-0 by Southampton. Gilzean, Kinnear and Knowles were all soon back in the line-up, but not Greaves. He was sidelined until Tuesday, 17 March – the day after the transfer deadline – when, in something of a rarity at the time, a football story was featured on the front page of the *Daily Mirror*.

The cover story announced that Greaves had been sold to West Ham, with World Cup winner Martin Peters going the other way. Spurs paid an additional £70,000, making Peters the most expensive player in British history.

The deal was registered with the Football League just 20 minutes before the deadline.

Peters told reporters, 'I think this is a good move for both Jimmy and myself.' Greaves was equally positive in the press, saying, 'It is tough leaving a great club like Spurs, but the time is right for the break.'

Nicholson had decided that, among other things, Greaves's drinking was out of control. Manchester City, Crystal Palace and Ipswich had all tried and failed with bids for Greaves, before the deal with West Ham was struck. Greaves had told friends that he would accept a transfer if Spurs wanted to sell him.

Peters had issued a transfer request at Upton Park in October, saying, 'I feel I have reached the point of no return with West Ham.'

Greaves's departure was made bitter by the bluntness of Spurs' treatment of him. Not for the last time, a Tottenham icon was allowed to leave without ceremony. He felt he had been disposed of, and there developed a rift between him and the club's hierarchy which took many years to be fully healed.

Greaves left as comfortably the club's greatest goalscorer, with 268 goals in 381 appearances across nine seasons. He hadn't been capped for England since May 1967, but finished his international career with the sensational record of 44 goals in 57 appearances and was the country's second highest goalscorer, behind only Bobby Charlton. He had just passed his 30th birthday and, in happier circumstances, could still have played on for club and country.

Perhaps in another era, Greaves would have received the help he needed to deal with his off-field problems and the great Chivers-Greaves partnership envisioned by Nicholson might have come to fruition. But it was not to be.

His departure was controversial among the players, too. Decades later, Jennings remains adamant that, despite the brilliance of Peters, the sale of Greaves was a mistake.

It seemed like the end, but actually signalled the dawning of Nicholson's second great team. The signing of Peters knitted together the brilliance of Chivers with the rest of the players. The 1966 World Cup winner was the catalyst, the final addition required to bring together all Nicholson's careful building. For Chivers, it meant no longer playing the supporting role to Greaves, telling reporter Bob Harris at the time, 'Now that Jimmy has gone I am playing a definite role. Instead of taking the weight off him, I am now an outright striker.'

Another quietly significant moment of the season was the debut of 17-year-old Steve Perryman in a September defeat to Sunderland. Perryman's intelligence, energy and flexibility would make him a vital player over the next 17 years in which he collected a club record 854 appearances and six trophies, as well as staying to endure the catastrophic late 1970s.

With Perryman joining Mullery in midfield, Spurs had a platform for Peters and Chivers to perform on. On 13 April 1970, two days after Paul McCartney announced that the Beatles had broken up, Tottenham beat Manchester United 2-1 at White Hart Lane. Greaves was gone and the Beatles were no more; the 1960s were well and truly over.

The success of a team committed to attacking football above all was a step into a new era for British football.

For the first time, Nicholson faced real pressure as Tottenham manager. Some journalists and even some fans thought his time was up and called for him to leave the club. Three seasons without a trophy, the controversial departure of Greaves, and the relative lack of success of the most recent signings fuelled that criticism. The fact that Nicholson had never had a contract at Tottenham – he simply worked on a handshake deal with the chairman – meant that removing him would have been easy to do.

Virtually allergic to publicity, Nicholson refused to publicise just how hard he worked and how much he sacrificed for the club. While it was not a majority of fans, there was a vocal minority that wanted a new manager.

The People wrote, 'Spurs – ravaged by tragedy, injuries and the advancing age of a once-great team – now battle a peril on their own terraces.'

One cause for optimism came in the FA Youth Cup. In August 1969 Nicholson had appointed former England youth coach Pat Welton to run Tottenham's youth system. Double winner Ron Henry, who had retired three years earlier, also joined as Welton's assistant.

With Nicholson having identified the glaring need for home grown talent – in light of the evolution of the transfer system – he had turned to Welton. Welton had guided England's under-18s to victory in the UEFA European Under-18 Championship – nicknamed the 'Little World Cup' – in 1963 and 1964. His teams also finished as runners-up in 1965 and 1967.

'Bill felt the club wanted to concentrate more on youth and that is why he brought me in. My job is all about getting people into the first team and it's satisfying to see players winning places on merit,' Welton said.

The FA Youth Cup had been conceived much earlier, with the trophy even being purchased during the Second World War, but it was first launched in 1952.

Manchester United won the first five editions. Their emerging young stars – the future Busby Babes – got their first experience of winning trophies, and they developed a taste for it.

In 1970, under the guidance of Welton, Tottenham won it for the first time. Future first-team players like Barry Daines, Mike Dillon, Steve Perryman and Graeme Souness led Spurs to the trophy after a final that had to be replayed twice against Coventry City.

7

The trophy drought ends

THE 1970/71 season is remembered as a famous one for the other north London club, with Arsenal winning both the First Division and FA Cup, but it was also the year Spurs finally found their feet again.

Over the summer youngsters Terry Naylor and Jimmy Neighbour were promoted to the first-team squad and Spurs started the season well.

Martin Chivers, who had never yet quite been loved by the Tottenham fans, had a breakthrough moment in October. He scored an excellent goal against Stoke City, one of two in a 3-0 win, bending the ball past England goalkeeper Gordon Banks.

White Hart Lane erupted and Chivers always remembered that as the moment he truly rediscovered his confidence following that brutal knee injury.

Despite a 2-0 defeat to Arsenal at Highbury in September, Tottenham were just two points behind table-topping Leeds United in late November. An almost-traditional winter slump followed, though, as they took just four points from their next six games. They were 11 points off the pace on 1 January, but upset Leeds 2-1 at Elland Road a few days later with Chivers scoring both goals.

Rather than bringing themselves back into the title race however, Spurs had opened the door for Arsenal. Tottenham's eternal rivals then claimed the first half of their Double with a 1-0 win at White Hart Lane. Arsenal were league champions for the first time in 18 years and, having won the title at Spurs' ground, they snatched an everlasting source of bragging rights.

In the FA Cup, Tottenham started quite well. Sheffield Wednesday were swept aside 4-1, Carlisle United were edged out 3-2, and Nottingham Forest were beaten 2-1.

The quarter-final draw pitched Spurs at Liverpool. They got a rare result at Anfield, drawing 0-0 to set up a replay at White Hart Lane. Over 56,000 fans packed the Lane to see an excellent Spurs performance in the second fixture. Despite the injury-enforced absence of Gilzean, Tottenham played on the front foot. Chivers and Alan Mullery might both have had penalties, while Martin Peters and John Pratt each went close to scoring.

John Toshack headed down for Steve Heighway to put the visitors in front but Spurs continued to attack bravely. Not for the first time, nor the last, future Tottenham goalkeeper Ray Clemence played brilliantly as Liverpool snatched the result 1-0. They would go on to lose in the final to Arsenal.

Spurs' best performances that season came in the League Cup. Swansea City were beaten 3-0, then Sheffield United were seen off 2-1. West Bromwich and Coventry City were hammered 5-0 and 4-1 respectively to set up a two-legged semi-final against Second Division side Bristol City, which was won 3-1 on aggregate, and Spurs had secured a date at Wembley against Aston Villa. Villa were in the Third Division at the time, though they eliminated Manchester United in the semi-final.

After a tight first half at Wembley, Willie Anderson hit the bar for Villa and it briefly seemed as though an upset might be brewing. Andy Lochhead thought he'd scored for the Midlands side, shooting towards an empty net after Jennings's collision with defender Peter Collins, but Steve Perryman somehow got back in time to clear it.

Spurs weathered the Villa storm before Chivers took over. Dwarfing defenders and dominating in the air, Chivers could be an absolute battering ram of a forward, but his performance against Villa showed all his rich skills. For Spurs' opening goal he nodded down a Phil Beal long ball to Alan Gilzean who turned and played it to winger Jimmy Neighbour. Neighbour's shot was saved but fell to Chivers who calmly fired it into the bottom corner.

Chivers' second goal was magnificent and long-remembered as a classic. Racing beyond the battered Villa centre-halves, Chivers took down a pass on the run, artfully turned between two defenders in the box and rolled it into the goal with his left boot.

Bill Nicholson, usually so sparing in his praise, admitted that Chivers 'won us the game today'. Chivers joked after the match that his manager had 'gone mad' to be so lavish with his praise.

Spurs had ended their short trophy drought and finished a respectable third in the league. More success would swiftly follow.

Victory against Villa at Wembley brought with it entry into two different competitions.[9] European football's newest tournament, the UEFA Cup (often pronounced 'oofa' in television coverage of the era), awaited Nicholson's side but first there was the Anglo-Italian League Cup. The short-lived tournament pitted one of the two cup winners from England against the Coppa Italia champions.

Torino were Spurs' opponents and Chivers was once again the star, scoring the only goal in Turin and another in the return leg at White Hart Lane as Nicholson's men won 3-0 on aggregate.

---

9   Tottenham became the first team to qualify for European football by winning the League Cup. Negotiations between the Football League and UEFA – in which the Football League threatened to boycott the UEFA Cup entirely – yielded a change in the rules.

In the UEFA Cup, Spurs' first opponents were Icelandic side Keflavík, who were thrashed 6-1 away from home and 9-0 at White Hart Lane. An 18-year-old Graeme Souness made his only appearance for Spurs in the first leg.

Next was a tricky tie against Nantes which Spurs edged 1-0, with Martin Peters scoring the only goal in London.

With Real Madrid and Juventus in the draw for the third round, Tottenham instead came out against Romanian side Rapid București and dispatched them 5-0 on aggregate. Peters scored after 20 seconds of the first leg at White Hart Lane following a long throw by Chivers, who was once again the star for Spurs, scoring three goals in the tie.

The second leg was so violent that the local authorities wouldn't allow the recordings of the match to be taken back to Britain for broadcast. Half the team was on the treatment table, Alan Gilzean went off injured, and Jimmy Pearce got sent off.

A second Romanian team followed in the quarter-final, Unizale Textile Arad, who were beaten 3-1, then Italian giants AC Milan were Spurs' next opponents, finally providing the glamour tie that a European run was supposed to ensure.

The first leg was their eighth game in 19 days, but the exhausted side put on an excellent performance, possibly the greatest in Europe under Nicholson. Steve Perryman scored a rare brace in a first-leg win, before Alan Mullery sealed victory with a goal at the San Siro.

Mullery had endured a trying season. Despite being captain, a recurring stomach injury had seen him lose his place in the starting line-up and he was eventually sent out on a mid-season loan to Second Division Fulham. His goal against Milan was a cathartic moment of redemption.

Wolverhampton Wanderers had beaten Hungarian side Ferencváros in the other semi-final, meaning the first UEFA Cup Final would be an all-English affair. Yet again, Chivers was the man to whom Spurs looked. Almost immediately after kick-off, Ralph Coates won a free kick on the edge of Wolves' penalty area and Chivers stepped up to deliver an almighty strike, but his shot clattered into the post and out of play.

Minutes later, Chivers' perfectly timed run split the Wolves defence and he rose well but placed his header uncharacteristically wide. Before half-time the big striker had another chance to open the scoring but blazed his shot over the bar.

Finally, after almost an hour of play, Mike England's free kick floated invitingly into the box and Chivers leapt to head home. Wolves equalised but ten minutes from time Chivers scored perhaps the greatest goal of his career. Taking down a long Jennings punt near the left touchline, Chivers took off and belted an unstoppable strike from more than 30 yards out.

Spurs took a 2-1 lead back to White Hart Lane, where Mullery scored again to seal another European trophy. At the final whistle, the fans flooded the pitch and lifted Mullery on to their shoulders, parading the match-winner on a lap of honour.

It marked the culmination of Mullery's journey from unfairly maligned 'replacement' for the irreplaceable Danny Blanchflower to a Tottenham legend in his own right.

Mullery left that summer. He went back to Fulham for £65,000, only £7,500 less than Spurs had paid in 1964. Mullery called it 'a wrench' to leave White Hart Lane. He was very disappointed and said he knew Nicholson had made a mistake.

In the summer, a concession was made to modernity with advertising hoardings finally being introduced around the pitch at White Hart Lane. While other stadiums had had them for decades, Spurs had resisted the urge to cheapen their home ground with advertisements, but generally poor economic conditions prevailed over philosophy. The club's total income in 1972 had been just £500,000. A new £26,000 floodlight system was also unveiled for the new campaign, replacing the original lighting installed in 1953.[10]

In June 1972 England lost to West Germany at Wembley in an infamous European Championship quarter-final. Chivers and Peters started as the English national team's greatest era came to a sudden end.

While England were no longer world champions – Brazil had succeeded them in 1970 – they retained the psychological notion that they were the world's finest team. The defeat two summers later brought the curtain down brutally upon that idea. Parallels were drawn with the 1953 humiliation at the hands of the 'Magnificent Magyars', the Hungarian team that dominated international football in the early 1950s.

On this occasion, Chivers and Peters were made to look ordinary, playing an outdated style on the biggest stage.

Neither player's international career was ended by the disaster at Wembley. There was a national reckoning, but it took place away from the team. It was more of a psychological wound than the impetus to enact real change.

Manager Sir Alf Ramsey clung on to his job, despite the evidence that it was past time for a change, and not until the disastrous failure to qualify for the 1974 World Cup would Ramsey be replaced.

The 1972/73 season brought a similar return to the previous one for Tottenham, and their league campaign was indifferent at best.

John Pratt scored a sensational goal in an early match against Wolves – so good that it was one of four nominated for *The Big Match*'s goal of the season award at the end of the year – but Spurs lost by the odd goal in five.

---

10 The first match under lights at White Hart Lane was a friendly against five-times Coupe de France champions Racing Club de Paris in September 1953.

A highlight was the Jimmy Greaves testimonial. After leaving Tottenham to join West Ham, Greaves had lasted for just one season at Upton Park.

His 13 league goals for the Hammers took his career total to 357 – still the all-time record for English top-flight goals by some margin – but off-field issues undermined his form and fitness. By the end of that campaign, he was finished as a footballer at the highest level.

Feyenoord were lined up as opponents for the match – and received a £3,000 appearance fee – and Greaves returned to Tottenham's training ground for the first time in 30 months to prepare.

Three minutes after kick-off at White Hart Lane, in front of 45,799, Greaves had already scored a typically brilliant goal. The match finished 2-1 to Tottenham and Greaves gave his team-mates a generous gift of £100 each out of the proceeds.[11]

Spurs were level at the top of the First Division with Arsenal and Liverpool after ten games, and only four points off the leaders in November, but had a terrible run in December and finished eighth.

Another bitter blow in December was the departure of Graeme Souness. Scotsman Souness had joined the club as an apprentice in 1968. He was desperate for first-team action, but Nicholson was insistent that young players had to win their place.

Mullery wrote years later that Nicholson believed Souness would be Dave Mackay's replacement at the heart of his team. However, Souness's homesickness was too much for him. It broke Nicholson's heart but the manager let him leave, selling Souness to Middlesbrough for £30,000.

Souness considered it 'an unbelievably kind gesture' and went on to have a historic career, winning five league titles and three European Cups at Liverpool alone.

---

11 The exact amount that Greaves received is unknown. Greaves scoffed at rumours that his contemporary Bobby Moore got around £30,000 for his own testimonial.

Tottenham made a fine run at defending their UEFA Cup, losing to eventual winners Liverpool on away goals in the semi-final. Once again, Ray Clemence starred against the club he would later represent 240 times in the First Division.

In May, Martin Chivers faced Pat Jennings as England beat Northern Ireland 2-1 at Goodison Park. Chivers scored both goals, pouncing on an error from opposition player-manager Terry Neill for the winner.

In light of the difficult relationship the two men would endure in the years to come, Chivers always wondered if Neill remembered that moment.

In the League Cup, Spurs knocked Liverpool out in the quarter-final, winning 3-1 in a replay. As ever, the talismanic Chivers scored twice.

Chivers and Peters both scored in the semi-final second leg as Spurs knocked out Wolves to secure another trip to Wembley and a meeting with Norwich City.

It was Tottenham's fifth trip to the Empire Stadium under Nicholson, and they had yet to taste defeat.

8

Ralph Coates's broken dream
comes true

RALPH COATES'S Tottenham career was at a crossroads. Signed in May 1971, following the relegation of his boyhood club Burnley, Coates had failed to really deliver on his promise.

As an uncapped player, Coates had narrowly missed out on selection for the 1970 Mexico World Cup. He was named in the 28-man travelling England squad but was cut from the final group.

He had starred for the Clarets – helping to keep them up as their star and midfield playmaker – and Spurs had moved quickly to sign him at the end of the 1970/71 season. Notably, Double winners Arsenal had also been interested but Tottenham had moved faster.

Coates had cost £190,000 – more money than any player in British football up to that point – and Nicholson had promised him the number seven shirt. He had been something of a qualified success, admitting himself that he was 'embarrassed' by the transfer fee that Spurs had paid for him. He initially struggled, but after asking to play in midfield – rather than as a traditional winger – Coates began to impose himself more on the team.

For six weeks in the lead-up to the League Cup Final, Coates had been struggling for fitness. Three days before

Spurs faced Norwich City he was asked to play for the reserves to prove he was ready for Wembley.

At a near deserted White Hart Lane, Coates – Spurs' record signing at the time – faced Swindon Town and set up one goal in a 4-0 win. Afterwards, Coates admitted that he felt that he had been made 'the scapegoat' for a 5-3 FA Cup defeat at home to Derby County a month earlier.

Having done what he could to prove form and fitness against Swindon, Coates added, 'Now it's in the lap of the gods whether I play in the final.' He was desperate to do so, saying, 'The only reason I left Burnley was so I could join a club with a chance of major honours. Tottenham were that kind of club. I collected a UEFA Cup winners' medal last season but, let's face it, there's nothing like a Wembley final.'

Prophetically, Coates thought he could be the difference-maker, 'I feel it would be the start of proving what I can do.'

Jimmy Pearce was struck by food poisoning four days before the match – he blamed 'a bad Chinese meal' – and it seemed certain that Coates would get his chance. But Pearce recovered and Nicholson declined to pick Coates.

Sticking with the form team, Nicholson also preferred Joe Kinnear to Ray Evans in defence, despite Evans having played every match of the cup run so far.

As the players walked out at Wembley – with Spurs wearing yellow socks – as they also did in the final against Villa in 1971 – Coates took his seat on the bench. The winger was bitterly disappointed, and newspaper reports after the match suggested that he would have been considering a transfer request.

But 23 minutes into the match, with the scores still level and Norwich packing the backline, John Pratt was forced off with an ankle injury. Nicholson turned to Coates, and the former Burnley man – with his famous combover flapping in the breeze – strode on to the pitch.

Norwich had been struggling in the league, indeed they were fighting relegation and would finish 20th, but they had knocked out Leicester, Arsenal and Chelsea en route to the final.

The Canaries had never before been to Wembley. They had won the League Cup in 1962, but that final – against Rochdale – had been played home and away over two legs. They rose to the occasion though, and Spurs had not dominated as expected.

The introduction of Coates helped swing the match. Racing down the right wing, he came close to a first-half assist and he also defended bravely on the edge of his own box.

Coates set up another chance for Spurs early in the second half with an exciting run but Pearce's shot hit the post and ran wide. The substitute moved into midfield as the game went on, driving his team forward while still making those exciting runs.

With 20 minutes to play, a long throw from Chivers created chaos in the Norwich box. The Canaries half cleared but Coates arrived at the top of the box and fired a low shot with the outside of his right boot into the bottom corner.

The match had not been the spectacle that the 100,000-strong crowd had hoped for but Norwich came close to earning a second attempt at winning the trophy but missed a late chance.

Afterwards, Canaries captain Duncan Forbes argued that his team had been deserving of at least forcing a replay, but Tottenham had hit the post three times and had several other good chances well saved, while Norwich had only one real opportunity to speak of.

Captain Martin Peters lifted the trophy alone but he invited Coates to help him carry it around the pitch in recognition of his major contribution to another piece of silverware heading to White Hart Lane.

After the match, Coates was philosophical, saying, 'I've been disappointed ... I haven't settled in as well as I'd hoped. I haven't clicked as I know I can with Spurs ... it's funny how fate takes a hand.'

Coates, who had been on the verge of giving up on making it at Tottenham, would stay for five more seasons and make 300 appearances for the club before joining Leyton Orient on a free transfer.

The latest trophy meant a third successive UEFA Cup campaign. It would, however, be Spurs' last venture into European football for ten years.

9

Return to Rotterdam

THE 1973/74 season, the last of Bill Nicholson's 15 full campaigns as Tottenham manager, began disastrously.

Before a ball was even kicked, Spurs faced an injury crisis. Winger Jimmy Pearce, who had played 44 games the previous season and scored nine goals, was sidelined and would eventually be forced to retire due to a knee problem. Young defender Peter Collins, still a squad player at the time but seen as Mike England's long-term replacement, also faced the same fate.

Nicholson had had high hopes for Collins, travelling personally to sign him as a young professional on the same day he closed the £125,000 Martin Chivers deal in 1968. After scoring the final goal of Tottenham's 1972/73 season, Collins had suffered an ankle injury.

Initially misdiagnosed, Collins too would never play for Tottenham again.

England and Terry Naylor were also both unavailable for Tottenham's final warm-up matches. The last of those, a friendly against European champions Ajax, offered a chastening glimpse into the team's readiness for the new campaign, which was two weeks away. Spurs were hammered 4-1; Johan Cruyff scored two goals in as many minutes as Ajax raced into a 4-0 lead after just 32 minutes. Martin Peters did pull one back in the second half but there was little else for Spurs to smile about.

Nicholson's squad was badly depleted and he also found it impossible to find value in the transfer market. Once one of his greatest strengths as a manager, Nicholson was constantly frustrated by what he saw as a lack of quality in available players. It was an issue which would persist and help pave the way towards his eventual departure.

Things only got worse when the season actually got underway. A 1-0 defeat to Coventry City – who had battled relegation the previous season – augured poorly for the campaign to come.

The previous season had opened with the reverse fixture. Tottenham had won that day 2-1 at White Hart Lane, but this time around Nicholson's depleted side managed to avoid a hammering only thanks to Jennings's heroics.

Nicholson had made the unusual decision to deploy Alan Gilzean in a defensive covering role – essentially as an extra full-back to stop Scotland midfielder Tommy Hutchison – but that just left Chivers isolated. This was something of a betrayal of Nicholson's ideals.

Never one to sacrifice flair for defensive solidity, did asking Gilzean to drop deep reveal a loss of confidence for the Tottenham manager?

A week later they were thumped 3-0 by Leeds United at White Hart Lane. Don Revie had come close to leaving Leeds the previous season, but having stayed he was building a mighty team. They had opened the campaign at Highbury, playing so well that the Arsenal fans applauded them off after their 2-1 win.

At Spurs, Leeds had the game won inside 25 minutes. Later, Ralph Coates took an elbow to the face from Billy Bremner and his white shirt was soaked with blood.

Renovations to White Hart Lane – the West and South stands were linked for the first time – had added another 700 seats to the ground's capacity over the summer, and over 42,000 came out for the Leeds match.

By the end of the campaign the crowds had halved. Only 20,110 attended on the final weekend of the season, a 1-0 win against Leicester City.

A week after losing to Leeds, Spurs were beaten again – at home to Burnley by the controversial odd goal in five. They had produced their best performance of the season so far and were leading 2-1 with 20 minutes to play when both Coates and Alan Gilzean had separate penalty appeals turned down in quick succession. Captain Martin Peters had to be restrained by his team-mates when, a few minutes later, Burnley were awarded a penalty of their own before adding a winner shortly afterwards.

The controversy led the coverage of the match and the referee was booed off the pitch, but Tottenham's woeful start to the season went on and by Christmas they were 17th. The only highlight of their league campaign was doing the double over Arsenal.

They were bounced out of both cups at the first time of asking, losing 1-0 to Queens Park Rangers in the League Cup and Leicester in the FA Cup.

But still, there was Europe. Nicholson had famously said of European football, following the 1967 FA Cup Final win over Chelsea, 'It's magnificent to be in Europe, and this club – a club like Tottenham Hotspur – if we're not in Europe … we're nothing. We're nothing.'

Grasshopper Club Zürich were Spurs' first opponents in the UEFA Cup, the Swiss club hammered 5-1 at home and 4-1 in the return leg. Nicholson was so confident ahead of the second leg that he gave reigning FWA Footballer of the Year Pat Jennings the night off, selecting 22-year-old Barry Daines for just his fifth Spurs appearance.

Nineteen-year-old winger Chris McGrath scored twice in a second-leg win over Aberdeen, sealing a 5-2 aggregate success over the Scottish side in the second round. Eyebrows were raised by the poor crowd in the second leg at White

Hart Lane. Despite the result being completely in the balance after a 1-1 draw at Pittodrie, only 21,785 fans were in attendance.

Dinamo Tbilisi earned a first-leg draw in the Georgian capital but were crushed in London in the second leg of the third round. Chivers and Peters each scored twice, either side of another McGrath goal. Once again, despite the outcome of the tie being in doubt, only an unimpressive 18,000 supporters bought a ticket.

Spurs were in the quarter-final and looked imperious ahead of their meeting with West Germany's Cologne. They had been runners-up in the Bundesliga and DFB-Pokal the previous season so were no lightweights but Spurs won 2-1 in Germany, and 3-0 at home to roll into the semi-finals.

In the last four they avoided the other West German side in the draw – Stuttgart – but landed the East Germans Lokomotive Leipzig.

Lokomotive had dumped Bobby Robson's Ipswich Town out in the previous round, proving themselves worthy contenders. After all, Spurs had failed to beat Ipswich in their last five attempts.

Days before the first leg, *The People* published an article headlined 'Spurs seek new boss'. The story argued that Nicholson had taken the decision to leave himself, and that the poor league season was not the reason.

Dave Mackay, Gordon Jago and Jimmy Bloomfield were named as the three candidates, with Tottenham's board apparently seeking to avoid any 'complications and recriminations'. Spurs denied the report, but it was the first indication of what was to come.

Just shy of 75,000 East Germans packed the Zentralstadion for the biggest match in Leipzig's history. Only 150 Spurs fans were permitted to enter the Soviet Bloc country, and they were compelled to surrender their passports and cameras upon arrival.

Despite the ferocious atmosphere, Tottenham charged into a 2-0 first-half lead courtesy of goals from Peters and Coates. Leipzig pulled a goal back but Spurs had done the hard work.

Back in London, Chivers scored a typically excellent goal, receiving possession on the edge of the box and striding past lunging defenders before lashing it into the net. The young McGrath scored again, the final goal in a 4-1 aggregate win.

There were three league matches to play but all focus was on the UEFA Cup Final. Feyenoord had beaten Stuttgart 4-3 on aggregate to secure their place as Spurs' opposition.

Tottenham's final league match of the season was a routine victory against Newcastle United, which would prove to be Alan Gilzean's final appearance for the club.

On the same day, Tottenham won the FA Youth Cup again. Neil McNab and Chris Jones, two players who would be important in the club's immediate future, were the stars of the team as they beat Huddersfield 2-1 over two legs.

With European glory on the horizon, and a thriving youth team, both the present and the future seemed to be in good hands.

Bill Nicholson had reached 11 finals and won them all, although through their entire run in Europe that season Spurs had played the away leg first, with the advantage of knowing exactly what was required in the home leg. For the final, they would play at home first and the decisive away leg second.

Dutch side Feyenoord had won the Eredivisie nine days before the first leg of the final. Five of their starting 11 had won the European Cup four years earlier, beating Jock Stein's Celtic 2-1 at the San Siro.

Seven of them would be in the Netherlands squad for the upcoming World Cup in West Germany, where they would become known as one of the finest teams in international football history, though they would lose the final 2-1 to the hosts.

The fans finally turned out in force for the first leg of the final, with a crowd of 46,281 seeing Mike England head Spurs into the lead after McGrath won a free kick out wide before a brilliant free kick from Willem van Hanegem equalised for the Dutch side before half-time.

England thought he'd added another just after the hour mark, but defender Rinus Israël got the last touch and was awarded an own goal.

A 2-1 win would have been a solid result for Spurs but Theo de Jong ran on to an excellent through ball to equalise shortly before full time. As a negative for the Dutch side, Van Hanegem, Feyenoord's number ten and one of their finest players, was booked during the match and would miss the second leg.

On the same day that Tottenham drew with Feyenoord, they agreed a very significant transfer. Nicholson had convinced Queens Park Rangers manager Gordon Jago to swap Chivers for fellow England striker Stan Bowles.

Nicholson liked Bowles and was completely fed up with Chivers. The deal was all set to go through but QPR's chairman stepped in and vetoed it at the last minute.

While Chivers stayed and continued to score regularly for Tottenham, his difficult relationship with Nicholson wouldn't be mended for years to come.

Bowles, though, was no angel and frequently clashed with his managers. Bowles had helped lead QPR to second in the First Division in 1975/76 but he later fell out with managers Tommy Docherty and Brian Clough as well as openly drinking, gambling and cavorting. The Rs dealt with their unsettled squad by dumping Terry Venables at Crystal Palace. Shortly afterwards, Bowles withdrew his transfer request.

Meanwhile, Spurs had the second leg of a cup final to worry about. The build-up hinted at the trouble that was to come. Spurs fans crossing the Channel on ferries threw fire extinguishers overboard. Supporters destroyed train carriages and smashed shop windows in Rotterdam all while clashing with police.

Fans had piled into the old green and white coaches at Stamford Hill and unloaded on streets already strewn with wreckage, with followers of both clubs fighting during and after the match.

The occasion was the final assignment in the long career of Italian Concetto Lo Bello, who had refereed England's 1966 World Cup win against Mexico as well as the 1968 and 1970 European Cup finals. Lo Bello still holds the record for most Serie A matches refereed at 328. He also took charge of 93 international matches and the 1960 Olympic football final, which was won by Yugoslavia over Denmark. There was arguably not a better-qualified referee in Europe to handle a match of this magnitude.

Ten minutes after kick-off, McGrath raced on to a long forward ball and took a touch around onrushing goalkeeper Eddy Treijtel. McGrath steadied himself and shot into the net from a wide angle, only for the referee to blow for offside. The Tottenham supporters – already simmering – boiled over. The fence dividing them from the home fans was torn down and a huge brawl spiralled quickly out of control. Baton-wielding riot police charged the fans; over 200 were injured and 50 were arrested.

Long-time Tottenham Hotspur Supporters' Trust board member Pete Haine remembers the atmosphere being truly frightening. It was unlike anything he ever experienced at a match before or since. He summed it up years later, saying simply, 'it was not an experience I wish for again'.

The Tottenham players later admitted it was difficult to continue playing as they watched the violence in the stands.

Feyenoord, with the advantage of their away goals, were content to sit back and play on the defensive while Spurs pushed forward. Three times a Ray Evans free kick found the head of a team-mate – first England, then twice Peters – but still Spurs couldn't find the breakthrough.

On 35 minutes Peters was fouled just outside the box after a slaloming run. He flicked the ensuing free kick over the Feyenoord wall for Phil Beal to run on to. Having caught Feyenoord completely by surprise, Beal was unmarked but slid his shot just wide of the post.

Minutes before half-time, Pat Jennings could only half clear a free kick and Feyenoord took the aggregate lead as Wim Rijsbergen scored. The goal sparked more violence in the Tottenham end, and once again the police charged the supporters in the upper deck of the stadium.

With Spurs trailing 1-0 at the break, Nicholson felt compelled to abandon his half-time team talk in favour of addressing the fans over the tannoy. He called the rioting supporters 'a disgrace to Tottenham Hotspur and England' as he begged them to stop.

When Nicholson returned to the dressing room, captain Peters saw tears in his manager's eyes. He and many others said afterwards that the actions of his own fans in Rotterdam contributed to what was soon to come.

By the end of half-time the crowd had been pacified, but the unpleasant mix of over-enthusiastic Dutch police, brawling fellow fans, and the shame brought on by Nicholson's words convinced many Tottenham supporters to leave before the second half. Some simply couldn't face any more.

Feyenoord scored again late in the second half to claim the UEFA Cup with a 4-2 aggregate win.

The match proved to be the end of the greatest period of Spurs' history, even if it wasn't immediately apparent. It was also a watershed moment for hooliganism.[12] The European Cup Final the following season would similarly be defined

---

12 Violent crime in the United Kingdom had been trending upwards since the mid-1950s but would not jump to its peak until the 1980s. The rising tide of violence carried football hooliganism along in its wake.

by the violence of Leeds fans in the streets of Paris. While football-related violence had been on the rise in the late 1960s and early '70s, Spurs' disgrace – coming on such a big stage – made front-page news in Britain, and images such as that of a Spurs fan on crutches being set upon by opposition supporters led the televised news coverage.

Following the violence in Rotterdam, Spurs were ordered to play their next two European matches 150 miles from White Hart Lane. But they did not look likely to be playing European football again soon – indeed they would not return to the continent until 1980.

They were left to face troubling realities. They had good players – including England stars like Peters and Chivers – but were now far from a top team. Their legendary manager was exhausted, physically and emotionally.

Manchester United had been, like Tottenham, a pillar of British football through the 1960s. England's first European Cup winners in 1968, United had been on a similar trajectory to Spurs and were relegated at the end of the 1973/74 season.

Part 2: The end of Bill Nicholson

10

The shifting ground

BILL NICHOLSON had won the league as a Tottenham player in Arthur Rowe's famous 'push and run' team in 1950/51. Rowe had played and coached in Hungary before the Second World War, working alongside the 'Golden Team' – the Hungarian stars who would dominate international football after the war with an aesthetically pleasing, attacking style. He brought the same attitude to Spurs, and passed it along in turn to Nicholson.

Vic Buckingham, a team-mate of Nicholson and a player under Rowe at Tottenham, carried those same ideals to Ajax and Barcelona where he helped lay the foundations for those clubs' own attacking philosophies. Buckingham was the coach who gave Johan Cruyff his debut at Ajax. Thus the two clubs with the most enduring footballing philosophies are part of the same lineage as Nicholson and the Double team.

Nicholson was famously restrained. He was rarely forthcoming with praise, preferring to see the flaws in a player or performance as part of an eternal search for footballing perfection.

His disposition then was diametrically opposed to his ideals. He was a footballing aesthete, for whom victory was not enough if it was not won in the 'right' way.

Rowe, Nicholson's predecessor, wanted his teams to entertain, to express themselves, to do more than just play to win. Nicholson had absorbed that attitude entirely.

As a player, Nicholson had not been able to express his ideas fully. He was a fine footballer, capped once for England, but his game lacked the beauty that he idealised.

Taking over in October 1958, Nicholson's first match was emblematic of his philosophy: Spurs beat Everton 10-4 at White Hart Lane. They scored after just two minutes, and led 6-1 at half-time.

After the match, Nicholson told the waiting press 'things can only get worse', while Everton were described as 'an incoherent mass of fumblers'.

Danny Blanchflower was magnificent that day. The midfield creator set up at least four of Spurs' ten goals, and Bobby Smith scored four alone.

Nicholson's second match was a similarly chaotic mix of brilliant attacking and underwhelming defending as Spurs beat Leicester, scoring four goals in a second-half comeback win.

After four matches in charge, Nicholson's team had both scored and conceded 16 goals.

Upon his ascension, Nicholson had about half of the Double-winning team already in place, but quickly added the final pieces.

In 1959 alone he signed Bill Brown, Dave Mackay, John White, Les Allen and Tony Marchi.

Scotland proved a fertile hunting ground for Nicholson. Goalkeeper Brown was signed from Dundee, Mackay joined from Hearts and White moved from Falkirk.

Les Allen was signed from Chelsea – where he was the strike partner of Jimmy Greaves – and Marchi was re-signed from Juventus two years after Tottenham had sold him.

The reforms to the transfer market benefited Spurs at first. Greaves and Marchi were brought in from Italy, where there was no wage cap, and Tottenham would not have been able to make a competitive offer under the old restrictions.

In building his great team, Nicholson had had the advantage of spending significant money – as he continued to do through the 1960s to sign the likes of Greaves, Martin Peters and Martin Chivers – but there was an emerging trend in the transfer market which troubled Nicholson.

More and more players were demanding under-the-counter payments in order to join – 'bungs' in the parlance of the time – but Nicholson steadfastly refused to go along. The board were entirely in agreement with their manager, absolutely unwilling to bend the rules in order to sign even a hugely promising player.

Given that restrictions on wages had been lifted, these payments were now in a slightly opaque area of the law. Clubs could pay players whatever they liked, but salaries were still supposed to be declared, and subsequently taxed.

The basic tax rate had fallen since the heights of the war but still remained high, at around 38 per cent until the early 1970s. The maximum rate was as high as 95 per cent – immortalised in the lyrics of the Beatles song, 'Taxman'.

While few footballers' basic wage would attract such a high level of taxation, signing-on bonuses were included and those could be substantial. With bonuses growing at a higher rate than either transfer fees or wages, this was the crucial point.

The institution of corporate tax for the first time in 1965 only complicated matters by creating an additional imposition on profits distributed to employees – including players contracted to football clubs. Thus, both players and clubs were incentivised to skirt the system.

Tottenham's refusal to engage in this grey market left them out of the running for the biggest names, and they were consequently compelled to buy lesser players for top fees.

The signing of Rangers midfielder Alfie Conn was an example of the effect of the changing landscape on Tottenham.

Signed for £150,000,[13] Conn would ultimately be a source of regret for Nicholson. He was a fine individual player, and gave occasional match-winning performances in his time at Spurs, but was unable to play the team-oriented game that Nicholson idealised. His Double team had been an automaton, pulling the opposition apart with movement and slick interplay, and Conn could not play that game. He was an individual.

Ironically, Spurs had scouted Conn for years at Rangers where he had been a controlling central midfielder.

Shortly before moving to Tottenham, Conn underwent surgery and lost more than two stone. After shedding the weight, the Scot became far more of a free spirit.[14] But his debut was delayed by his recovery.

Nicholson had wanted England midfielder Gerry Francis, and Ireland forward Don Givens – both from Queens Park Rangers – but was unable to close either deal so resorted to Conn instead.

There was another, perhaps equally significant factor. Tottenham simply were no longer an elite team.

As Wolverhampton Wanderers had been the team of the 1950s, so Spurs had taken their place in the 1960s. Tottenham had been the great team of the decade, perhaps the greatest British team of all. Certainly, they had done what had been considered impossible in winning the Double. They had been the first team since Aston Villa in 1897 to do so.

---

13 At the time Bob Latchford's transfer from Birmingham City to Everton for £350,000 was the British record while Johan Cruyff's £922,000 move from Ajax to Barcelona in 1973 was the world record. Spurs' own record signing at the time was Martin Peters, who had cost £200,000 when signed from West Ham in 1970, and Ralph Coates too had cost more than Conn but it was no small investment.

14 Years later, Luton manager David Pleat asked for Nicholson's thoughts on buying Conn. Nicholson responded that he could, but he would have to buy him his own ball, too. Conn's father, also Alfie, had played alongside Dave Mackay. Alfie junior had made his Rangers debut as a substitute, replacing Alex Ferguson.

When the vast differences in the footballing landscape between 1897 and 1961 are considered, it seems quite fair to rank Tottenham's achievement as something quite beyond that of Aston Villa, or indeed that of Preston North End who had done the Double themselves in 1889.

Preston – the original Lilywhites – went undefeated through every match they played that season in league and cup football, making themselves the only invincible team in British history.

However, despite that magnificent achievement, the late 1800s was a somewhat unrestricted period for football. In fact, Preston's insistence on paying amateurs to move to the club from Scotland – then considered the source of the most skilful players – had been a major factor in the creation of the Football League and the official professionalisation of the game.

Certainly, neither Villa nor Preston had to deal with a maximum wage as Spurs did. Given that the maximum wage was abolished in 1961, Tottenham's Double was the only one ever won on something approaching a level financial playing field.

Nicholson's team had achieved the impossible but they had fallen away. The financial developments came at the worst possible time for Spurs as they slipped from their previously vaunted position to something like a mid-table side.

Tottenham's decline played a role in their inability to recruit top players. Stars no longer saw Nicholson's Spurs as a place to go to enhance their careers. This also probably reinforced the other factor, with players likely wanting more illicit cash to join a club that they considered unlikely to further their careers. Without the guarantee of glory, financial incentives rose in importance.

Leeds, who had won two league titles and finished in the top three every year from 1969, had become unquestionably England's top team but the departure of manager Don Revie in July 1974 – and the infamous ensuing reign of Brian Clough – would see them similarly lose their place.

Spurs had continued to win trophies – they had won two League Cups, the UEFA Cup and the Anglo-Italian League Cup in the four seasons since they had last managed a sustained title challenge – but those successes had served only to obscure the fact that they were no longer a team to be feared.

Their identity had been the admired, hated and feared big-spending Londoners, but that had gradually eroded until the point that they were considered a 'cup team'.

Nicholson had never found a true replacement for Dave Mackay, a midfielder who could do everything and always knew exactly what a situation required. Danny Blanchflower and Cliff Jones had proven equally difficult to replace.

Jones, a winger who had scored 159 goals in ten years, is often left out of such discussion but his speed, grace, and magnificent aerial ability gave Nicholson's greatest team a weapon unmatched in later vintages.

Spurs were caught in a cycle of getting worse, and consequently being unable to get better. Nicholson could still spot stars, that skill would never leave him, but he was suddenly and irreversibly unable to get them to join his team.

11

Gathering clouds

AWAY FROM football, Britain was enduring its worst economic crisis since the Great Depression. Inflation was at 16 per cent and unemployment – a virtual non-factor since the Second World War – had begun to climb.

The proportion of the population living in poverty had doubled since the 1950s. Nearly ten per cent of the British population lived in poverty by 1973. The infant mortality rate, though steadily declining, remained roughly equivalent to that of the Gaza Strip in 2022.

Edward Heath's Conservative government's intensely unpopular Industrial Relations Act had provoked widespread labour strife in 1971.

The same government's refusal to increase miners' wages in line with other industries resulted in a six-week strike in 1972, crippling the country's capacity to generate electricity. The strike ended shortly after the Battle of Saltley Gate when 15 miners were injured by police and one, Fred Matthews, was killed by a non-union truck driver attempting to pass the picket line.

In response to the reduced energy production the government instituted the three-day week,[15] and a national maximum driving speed of 50 miles per hour was put in place.

---

15 Commercial users of electricity were restricted to only three days per week, with exceptions for hospitals and some other businesses.

Television broadcasting was shut down every day at 10.30pm, alternating nightly between ITV and the BBC. Driving was even banned on Sundays.

The economic turmoil generated political instability. Heath called a general election in 1974 on the issue of 'Who Governs Britain?'. The answer from the electorate was a comprehensive 'no one in particular'.

The two major parties received 37 per cent of the vote each, a combined total of fewer than 80 per cent for the first time since the Depression. Labour won more seats, 301 to the Conservatives' 297, but neither had a majority.

For four days in March the Conservatives tried to form a coalition with the Liberal party, but that failed and Harold Wilson's Labour became the a minority government. Labour's status necessitated a second election in October which returned a narrow majority for Wilson's party.

Amidst this turmoil, the extremist National Front party had emerged as a force in British political life, both informing and reflecting a hardening of British society. They stood the most candidates of any party outside the traditional parties in the national election that October.

While the Conservative right-wing politician Enoch Powell had given his infamous 'Rivers of Blood' speech six years earlier, opinion polls suggested that his views – namely that non-white immigration to Britain should be ended, and that non-white immigrants already present should be repatriated – remained popular.

Black footballers were becoming more common in the 1970s, and in this context the persistent racial abuse that they endured should come as little surprise.

The Troubles in Northern Ireland were at their height in 1974, too. Fifteen separate bombings occurred that year alone, causing over 80 deaths.

The grim Lord Lucan affair – in which a British peer was suspected of murdering his children's nanny before disappearing – captured the nation's attention in November.

The crime rate doubled from the 1960s to the 1970s, and the murder rate hit a historic peak in 1974.

Violence was not constant inside football grounds but, for those who wanted to seek it out, it could be found. In parks, trains, and pubs before and after matches, supporters of both sides would clash regularly.

Often the incidents in the stadium were not deliberate, instead the result of mixing home and away fans, but there were also often attempts to 'take' opposition areas of a ground.

For Tottenham fans, taking the North Bank at Highbury was a common target, and often resulted in violence.

On 24 August 17-year-old Blackpool fan Kevin Olsson became the first person to be killed inside a British football ground, stabbed to death in a historic flare of hooliganism. Nobody was ever charged in connection to his murder.

Football, being so central to the lives of so many, is always a reflection of society. The growing problem of football violence reflected a darkening of British life overall. The Christmas number one that year was the appropriately downbeat 'Lonely This Christmas'.

The gloomy pall cast across British life in 1974 provides the necessary context to understand both the violence of Tottenham fans in Rotterdam, and the momentous decision which Bill Nicholson would soon take.

Alan Gilzean had joined Tottenham from Dundee in December 1964. Just 26 years old, he had already scored 169 goals for the Scottish club. He worked as a clerk for a carpet company before turning professional, leading Dundee to their only Scottish league title in 1962. The next season saw him score five goals in their European Cup campaign, which ended with a semi-final defeat to eventual champions AC Milan.

After moving to Spurs, Gilzean quickly struck up a famous partnership with Greaves. The duo became known as 'The G-Men'.

Greaves described Gilzean as 'possibly the best footballer I ever played with'. *Times* writer Henry Winter, in a contemporary piece, opined, 'Few partnerships in English football can rival Greaves's balanced blend with Alan Gilzean.'

Gilzean had scored 133 goals in 439 games for Spurs, but after a season in which he made just 26 appearances, and was left out of both legs of the UEFA Cup Final, the Scottish veteran retired. He was the club's sixth-highest goalscorer, though he has since been surpassed by Chivers, Jermain Defoe and Harry Kane.

The Scot was the eighth member of the 1967 FA Cup winners to leave the club. That team had been the last of Nicholson's to mount a genuine title challenge. Gilzean briefly moved to South Africa, where he played for a short spell with Johannesburg club Highlands Park. Upon his return to England, Gilzean briefly got into management with Stevenage Athletic, but soon left football behind.

Nicholson was unable to find a replacement for Gilzean and so, frustrated at the lack of value in the transfer market, turned to youth instead. Keith Osgood, Matt Dillon and Jimmy Neighbour were promoted to fill the thin ranks of the first team.

Spurs began the new campaign at home to Ipswich. Chris McGrath, Osgood and Neighbour started, with Chivers, Phil Beal and John Pratt taken out of the line-up that had lost to Feyenoord 80 days earlier.

Not for the last time, Chivers had been transfer listed by Tottenham – the asking price was £250,000 – and had been dropped, while Beal was injured.

Before the match, Ipswich manager Bobby Robson admitted that Spurs were no longer a side to be feared, telling journalists, 'Once, a visit to White Hart Lane meant – at best – a point. That would have been a sort of triumph. But times change and we are looking for two points.' Ipswich, having succeeded Spurs as league champions in 1962, were still a strong side.

Young forward Chris Jones almost made a dream start but was denied a debut goal by a diving save.

David Johnson got the only goal, rising to head home a free kick conceded by Martin Peters. Peters had a late chance to equalise but couldn't score, summing up a performance described in *The People* as 'dismal'.

The newspapers had happily been reporting on Nicholson's 'Star Trek' as he travelled up and down the country in a desperate search for quality reinforcements. After the Ipswich match, Nicholson admitted that he had given up trying to buy his way out of trouble.

Allan Hunter, star centre-back for Ipswich and Northern Ireland, was announced as available for transfer the following day and Nicholson was seen as certain to bid. The 28-year-old was considered the best centre-half in England at the time and had refused Robson's pleas to extend his contract. He was available for £200,000.

Nicholson did attend Ipswich's next match, a 1-0 win against Arsenal at Highbury, and was widely assumed to be taking a final look at Hunter.

In the end Spurs did not make the widely anticipated move. Nicholson had once been so clear-minded and quick to act on transfers. He had pushed through deals for the likes of Jennings, White and Greaves with aggression and certainty. Had the defeat in Rotterdam, the battle with Chivers, the loss of so many reliable veterans undermined his confidence? Perhaps he was already wrestling with the decision that would soon shake the football world.

Ipswich had finished fourth the previous season and were entering the second of nine campaigns out of ten in which they would play European football, so there was no particular disgrace in being beaten by them. But it was the nature of the defeat – limp and ineffectual – that raised concern among supporters and the press alike.

More fan trouble occurred on the opening day as Manchester United faced Leyton Orient in the Second Division. Supporters were ejected from Brisbane Road and arrests were made, while broken glass had to be cleared off the pitch.

After losing their opener, Spurs next travelled to Manchester City. The youngsters kept their places and Chivers was still not selected. Again they lost by the only goal and again Peters missed a good late chance for an equaliser. City's winner was scored by £250,000 summer signing Asa Hartford, and while Spurs were struggling in Manchester, Chivers scored for the reserves.

Three days later Spurs faced promoted side Carlisle United at Brunton Park. Nicholson missed the match, away on a scouting trip to again watch Ipswich's Hunter, but it followed a familiar pattern against a team that had surprised observers by winning their opening two games.

Returning centre-back Mike England conceded a penalty. Jennings saved Chris Balderstone's spot-kick but the referee ordered it retaken and the midfielder scored on the second attempt. It was the only goal of the game, and Spurs had lost three straight, all 1-0.

Days after their latest defeat, Nicholson finally made a significant move in the transfer market. Struggling Spurs made a £300,000 offer for Burnley midfielder Martin Dobson. It would have made him the most expensive player in British history, but unbeknownst to Nicholson, Burnley had already agreed to sell Dobson to Everton for the same fee.

Dobson joined the growing list of players who Nicholson had tried and failed to sign that season. Celtic's Scotland midfielder David Hay had chosen Chelsea, moving in a £225,000 deal. Chelsea striker Bill Garner had also rejected

Tottenham, while Nottingham Forest forward Duncan McKenzie chose Brian Clough's Leeds.

On Wednesday, 28 August, just 11 days into the new season, Spurs faced Manchester City for the second time, this time at home.

Chivers was restored to the starting line-up and added the spark which had been missing. Although City scored first, Peters finally took a chance and equalised. It seemed that at least a point would be won, before disaster struck.

Chivers' back-pass – labelled 'inexplicable' in the press the following day – gave City the chance from which they scored a last-minute winner.

12

This is the end

FOUR GAMES, four defeats. Tottenham's worst start to a season since 1912. Bill Nicholson had seen enough. He gathered the board of the club he had served so well for so long and told them that he was finished. Although he had never technically had a contract, he asked that they release him from his position and allow him to resign.

The board agreed to Nicholson's request to be relieved of his duties and gave him a small bonus (between £5,000 and £15,000, according to various sources) to thank him for his service. One newspaper speculated that the bonus was two years' salary and added that it meant Nicholson had been the lowest-paid manager in the First Division.

Despite more than qualifying for one, Nicholson was not awarded a testimonial match. This decision would reverberate through Spurs' history for many years.[16]

Nicholson said of his decision to resign that while many factors – the violence in Rotterdam, the corruption within

---

16 Nicholson was compelled to 'sign on' at his local unemployment office shortly after his Tottenham exit. The board's mishandling of Nicholson's exit created a rift which lasted until 1976, when new manager Keith Burkinshaw invited Nicholson back to the club. Nicholson eventually got two testimonials, in 1983 and 2001, as well as having the road leading into White Hart Lane renamed Bill Nicholson Way. Upon his death in 2004, Nicholson's ashes were buried under the pitch at White Hart Lane. When the stadium was rebuilt in the 2010s, Nicholson was reinterred where the new and old pitches overlapped, during a private ceremony.

football, his complex relationship with Martin Chivers, the poor start to the season – had contributed, ultimately he was simply exhausted.

He admitted later that he would have resigned the previous summer had Spurs not been beaten in Rotterdam.

In a pre-season match against Fulham that summer, Nicholson had confided in Alan Mullery that he thought he had lost the respect of his players. Mullery, who had been angry with Nicholson after being sold two years earlier, was heartbroken by the state of the great man and instantly forgot their quarrel.

When asked by reporters why he was resigning, Nicholson said, 'It has become very difficult handling players and getting loyalty, respect and honesty from them.'

He admitted that the difficulties in buying new players meant that the process took far longer than it once had, shaving away the time he could spend with his squad, 'When I started as manager nothing got me away from training. I was with the players for most of the time and that way I got control and discipline.'

When the news reached the players, Peters and Beal went to Nicholson's office to ask him to reconsider. 'Change your mind. Withdraw your resignation. The players want you to stay,' the delegation told Nicholson.

Speaking with journalists, they repeated their pleas, saying, 'We wanted him to know we still have faith and confidence in him. We want him to know we would like him to stay.'

Nicholson's mind was made up, as he had already intimated to Mullery. He said again to Peters and Beal, 'Once you lose the respect of the players, you've got to pack it up.'[17]

---

17 Beal believes that one specific senior team-mate was responsible for Nicholson's loss of confidence, but refuses to name the player.

Nicholson had given everything to Tottenham Hotspur from the moment he was appointed manager in 1958, and by 1974 he was burned out and needed a break.

With Bill Shankly leaving Liverpool, and Ron Greenwood moving upstairs at West Ham, the old guard of managers was fading away. The postwar generation were moving on whether they wanted to or not.

Newspapers openly discussed that the fact that 'Honest Nick' refused to engage in under-the-table payments to convince players to move had been a significant factor. Nicholson claimed that requests for £10,000 – tax-free of course – were not uncommon.

Nicholson acknowledged that he was touched by the players' request that he change his mind and stay, but his mind was made up.

The board asked Nicholson to remain in his position until they could find a suitable replacement. He asked the players for their consent, which they happily gave, so he stayed on for a little longer. Midfielder John Pratt said afterwards, 'It was such a shock. We all thought that Bill would be at Tottenham forever.'

He nearly had been. Sixteen years had passed between the Everton win to start his tenure and the Manchester City defeat which finally brought the curtain down. No other English manager had stayed longer in a job since the war.

Nicholson had been at the club in some capacity for 38 years since joining the ground staff at the age of 17.

Just two days before Nicholson's resignation, chairman Sidney Wale had given an interview to the *Daily Mirror*, absolving the manager of any blame for the poor start, saying, 'The day will come when Bill says he wants to give up. I hope that day is a long way off. How do you replace a man like him?'

The day had come far sooner than Wale had hoped, and now he was forced to face the conundrum he had feared. How indeed could Spurs replace Bill Nicholson?

Nicholson thought there was an obvious replacement for him, already a fixture at the club. Double-winning captain Danny Blanchflower, who saw the game the same way Nicholson did, wanted to replace his former boss.

Days after resigning, Nicholson called Blanchflower. 'I interviewed him for the job of manager,' Nicholson later said. 'He wanted to know all the details and, after a long talk, he decided he'd like the job.'

Nicholson suggested signing Leeds' Johnny Giles as a senior influence on the pitch – the connection between manager and players. Blanchflower liked the idea and also wanted Nicholson to 'stay on in the background', which he would have been happy to do, forming a potentially ideal triumvirate.

From the day his resignation was made official, Nicholson had been clear that he wished only to stay on 'to assist, not to interfere'. Nicholson insisted, 'The new manager must be allowed to manage.'

For Nicholson, his own role was to be vital to the success of any new boss. The 'continental system' of dividing the manager's duties between one administrator in charge of contracts, and the practicalities of transfers and another focused on day-to-day management, was his favoured solution.

'It is very difficult to fight over contracts with a player and then take him out on the park for training,' Nicholson said, adding, 'I'm sure I took too much on myself at Spurs. I was involved in too many things when I should have been concentrating on the playing side.'

The players were excited by the idea of Blanchflower taking over, especially with Nicholson staying around.

Pat Jennings said, 'We were looking forward to Danny taking over as manager, and at Tottenham he would have had so much respect that it would have stood a good chance of working.'

After his chat with Nicholson, Blanchflower spent the afternoon playing golf with journalists and then returned home to wait for the inevitable phone call. He knew the Tottenham board were meeting that day, and assumed it was to confirm his appointment.

One fan, interviewed by *The People*, summed up the thoughts of many, saying, 'Danny's the only choice. All right, he's been out for ten years, but so had General [Charles] de Gaulle when he came back.'

Blanchflower saw the Tottenham job as a philosophical crusade, a chance to save football from itself. The Northern Irishman expounded on the golf course that day, explaining, 'We are all looking for genuine leadership. Better things to believe in. Football is important because it should provide an escape from frustration.'

He saw dwindling attendances as an inevitable consequence of the direction football was going in. He explained, 'The game bores the public, so they stay away.'

Blanchflower admitted that Nicholson had convinced him that it was his responsibility to step back into football after a decade outside the game, that he still had something more to contribute,

'I would like to make Spurs an academy for young players and that's where a large part of the effort would have to be put in.'

Despite having initially laughed at the idea of replacing Nicholson, Blanchflower was now intoxicated by the notion. But the call never came.

Instead, the board turned on Nicholson. Angered at what they perceived as a power grab – interviewing his potential successor without asking the board first – they refused his suggestions.

Years later, Nicholson told reporter Harry Harris, 'It was my opinion that [Danny] would have made an exceptional manager for the club, the outstanding candidate. He had similar ideas to mine about how the game should be played. He knew the setup and the tradition.'

Nicholson himself had passed from player, to coach, to manager. Later, successful Spurs bosses such as Keith Burkinshaw and Peter Shreeves would make similar transitions from backroom roles.

Tottenham's board had a chance to install continuity, maintaining the focus on style and attacking football that had proven so successful over more than a decade, but they opted for a different approach and Blanchflower was ruled out.

The directors justified this perplexing decision publicly by saying that Blanchflower had not applied for the job.

With all the difficulties looming just over the horizon, the decision not to go with Nicholson's suggestion of the Blanchflower-Giles tandem, with himself in a background role, must be considered one of the great sliding doors moments for Tottenham Hotspur.

The true reason for the board's refusal to appoint Blanchflower will never be known, but his iconoclastic nature would not have counted in his favour. Perhaps too, his absolute commitment to attacking football may have given pause to the conservative board members, running a club which faced a very real relegation battle.

Blanchflower himself had been revelling in the idea of taking charge at White Hart Lane, telling a journalist friend, 'Won't it be wonderful to take over a club and bring back real football?'

The appointment had been considered almost a certainty in the press. Once he was ruled out, other names began to be mentioned. Alf Ramsey, a league-winning Spurs team-mate of Nicholson in 1950/51, had just left his role as England manager and was among the first names linked. Derby County manager Dave Mackay, Allan Mullery – still playing at Fulham – and Queens Park Rangers boss Gordon Jago were all also mentioned as options.

With Spurs in a state of purgatory, Derby County arrived. Before the match, Nicholson was given a standing ovation by the White Hart Lane crowd. On his way into the ground the now caretaker manager was handed a Tottenham scarf and badge by young fans who told him they were 'retirement presents', which Nicholson declared 'marvellous'.

The script was written. Despite their team being bottom of the table and winless, the home crowd was buoyant and Tottenham won 2-0. Their first victory of the season, with two goals coming from promoted youngster Jimmy Neighbour, did not, however, convince Nicholson to change his decision.

Nicholson praised his players, saying that they 'certainly did me proud, we played some great stuff'. Chivers and Peters, retained in Nicholson's 11, could have run up the score against Derby but spurned their chances. Mackay, heavily linked with the open seat in the home dugout, admitted afterwards that he had been sure Spurs would beat his Derby team. John Pratt claimed bitterly that if the players had shown the same effort in previous matches as they had against Derby, Nicholson would still be the manager.

Former Manchester City manager and caretaker England boss Joe Mercer dedicated his newspaper column that weekend to a heavy criticism of the Tottenham players. He argued that they had failed Nicholson, not the other way around.

As the wait for a new manager went on, so too did Spurs' suffering on the pitch. They soon went to Anfield and were hammered 5-2. Mike England was forced off early in the second half with a back injury, leaving Tottenham once again threadbare in defence. The failure to sign Allan Hunter suddenly assumed even greater significance.

The next day, Johnny Giles devoted his regular column in the *Sunday Independent* to essentially interviewing himself for the Spurs job. He wrote of his pride at merely being considered for the job and laid out his strengths, including having played under Don Revie and his titles won with Leeds. He included the fact that he was still waiting for Spurs to call him.

Tottenham next suffered their worst home defeat in a decade, losing 4-0 to Middlesbrough in the League Cup. That day, former Spurs midfielder Graham Souness shone. Steve Perryman said his old team-mate was 'revelling in our discomfort'.

Alfie Conn, injured since his arrival from Scotland, finally made his debut in the Boro defeat, while Keith Osgood was carried off after fracturing his ankle.

Spurs were defenceless, and it showed. Their next game was the 5–2 hammering at Liverpool.

13

An Arsenal captain takes charge

THIRTY-TWO-YEAR-OLD Terry Neill was managing Hull City – mid-table in the Second Division at the time – as well as working part-time as the coach of Northern Ireland. He played 122 times for Hull in his role, usually in central defence, before ending his playing career and eventually managing the club 206 times.

That alone would make him an unusual choice to replace a living legend at White Hart Lane. What made it even more unusual was Neill's status as an Arsenal hero.

Neill had joined Arsenal in 1959 for £2,500 from Northern Irish club Bangor. He later scored the winner for Northern Ireland as they beat England 1-0 at Wembley in 1972.

He had spent 11 years playing for Spurs' greatest rivals and was, at the time he left Arsenal, their record appearance maker. His top-flight playing career had been undermined by a bout of jaundice and after losing his place in the Arsenal 11, he moved on to Hull.

En route to Norway with the Northern Ireland team, Neill decided to call Bill Nicholson and get the truth on the rumours of who would succeed him. Neill asked whether it was true that Johnny Giles and Danny Blanchflower would be taking over, as the press had reported.

Nicholson replied that it wasn't his call. The now former Tottenham manager had been under the impression that the board would follow his suggestion and hand the reins to the duo, but the directors were unhappy that he had acted without their express permission and rejected Nicholson's advice.

Neill got the story directly from Nicholson and admitted afterwards that it gave him pause. Neill asked himself; if Tottenham's board could mistreat their greatest legend in this fashion, what hope did he – a relative naif – have of dealing successfully with them?

When legendary Manchester United manager Matt Busby had resigned in 1969, he had remained in an official role at Old Trafford as general manager. Not only did he select his successor – Frank O'Farrell – but he also continued to play a direct role in the running of the club.

With United having been relegated the previous season and playing in the Second Division when Nicholson resigned, the prevailing wisdom was that the ongoing presence of Busby had been a mistake. With that in mind, chairman Sidney Wale and his fellow board members had no intention of allowing Nicholson to hand-pick the next manager. Not only was he denied that privilege, he was also denied any ongoing role at the club.

Nicholson was hurt by the nature of his exit, the rejection of his advice and the board's refusal to keep him on in a different capacity.

Soon afterwards, Ron Greenwood of West Ham gave him a job scouting players and he remained there until 1976.

Despite the unpleasantness of the board's conduct, Nicholson advised Neill to write to Wale if he wished to be considered for the job.

Wale contacted Hull chairman Harold Needler, and Needler – honouring an agreement he had with his manager – allowed Spurs to speak with him. The deal was sealed at an impromptu board meeting at Wale's house.

Neill himself was later unable to explain Tottenham's decision in choosing him to succeed Nicholson. At 32 he became the youngest manager in the First Division at the time. He had done reasonably well with Hull, but had hardly done the impossible, and he credited Nicholson's advice with getting him the job.

Years later, Neill reflected that perhaps he should have realised that his job was doomed to failure with an inflexible board which collectively knew little about the football world. He observed that board meetings were endless, dedicated to the minutiae of the club and interminable to sit through. Godfrey Groves, an older member of the board, occasionally nodded off.

If Neill's first job was navigating troubled waters with the board, his second was no less significant: dealing with the players.

He took Martin Chivers off the transfer list and began working on a new contract for the England striker, also promising to allow Chivers to go to Durban City to play as a guest in the summer. Chivers says Neill later reneged upon that deal.

Next he spoke with fellow unsettled players John Pratt and Mike Dillon, convincing them to withdraw their own transfer requests. Pratt had been offered to Luton in January in a swap deal for midfielder Alan West.

According to Brian Scovell's biography of Bill Nicholson, however, the squad were openly contemptuous of the choice to replace a legend with an untested youngster.

In an attempt to bond with the players, Neill took them and their wives and girlfriends to the Savoy Hotel for massages which served only to alienate several of the senior players.

One savvy move Neill made was to promote youth team manager Pat Welton to run the reserve team. With the club's finances in a less-than-ideal state, Spurs would come to rely on the production line of talent that Welton would oversee.

Neill and many of his players had a fractious relationship from the beginning. The new manager was six months younger than Mike England and had no major medals from his long playing career to point to. His attempt to convert the 33-year-old England and 29-year-old centre-back partner Beal to a zonal marking system was particularly unsuccessful. Beal and England went to see Neill, pleading to abandon the new defensive direction. Neill responded, 'if you can't do it, I'll get someone that can'.

In a departure from the ball-focused training sessions of Nicholson, Neill's target was fitness. He had his squad run in weighted vests, and packed away the balls. Once again, this served to upset his players. Neill would need instant results to win them to his way of doing things.

The new manager wanted to bring Alan Mullery – then 33 – back to the club from Fulham to provide leadership to a squad badly lacking it, but Mullery turned him down. The old Tottenham captain had been promised the manager's job at Craven Cottage, although he never got it. Instead Mullery took charge of Brighton & Hove Albion in 1976, where he eventually signed Chivers for a brief but successful spell.

Tottenham's supporters, too, were unimpressed by the decision, and Neill himself later said that there was a section of the fans that he knew he would never convince – regardless of his achievements – because of his Arsenal roots.

Reporter Harry Harris confronted Wale in the carpark after the announcement of Neill's appointment and asked him why the board had appointed an ex-Arsenal player. Wale responded that he was unaware of the connection.

Neill told a similar story of being taken aside by an unnamed board member during a club function and asked if the rumour that he had once played for Arsenal was true.

Neill did not endear himself to the fans with his relaxed attitude. Starkly contrasted to Nicholson's inexhaustible energy – working endless days and being on top of everything at the club – Neill had a far looser philosophy which he described as 'smiling through adversity'.

One of Neill's most significant contributions to Tottenham actually came in his first training session after being appointed.

As early as 1970/71, Steve Perryman had been playing on an injured ankle, and not showing his best form.

Early in Bill Nicholson's final season, the manager concluded that Perryman was not good enough. He decided to sell him. Chief scout Charlie Faulkner was in the room with Nicholson when he made the decision, and quickly called Perryman to warn him.

When Nicholson called Perryman to ask whether he would be willing to leave, the future Spurs captain said he would 'quite fancy a move'. Provided that Spurs could find him a club in London, near enough to his family home, he was willing to go.

It emerged that Perryman had been offered to Coventry City as part of a deal to sign midfielder Mick McGuire and defender Jimmy Holmes.

Nicholson asked Perryman again if he would go, and the player said he would. Negotiations began and continued until the infamous Manchester City defeat which signalled the end of Nicholson's time in charge.

In the confusion of Nicholson's resignation and the eventual appointment of Neill, Perryman's transfer was put on hold.

Perryman refused to sign Martin Peters' petition to ask Nicholson to stay, something he later called 'the most self-interested act of my career'.

At the end of his first day of coaching the team, Neill called Perryman over and asked, 'What's all this about you leaving?'

Evidently Nicholson or someone else at the club had filled him in on the ongoing negotiations with Coventry, but Perryman gave his own version. When he had finished, Neill simply said, 'You are not leaving this club.'

Perryman had already made about 270 appearances for Tottenham. After that discussion with Neill, he would make 600 more. His total of 866 games for Spurs is more than 250 higher than any other player. In all the tumult that was to come, Perryman would be the sole survivor.

The Terry Neill era at White Hart Lane officially began on 14 September 1974 with Tottenham bottom of the First Division, a squad riven by divisions, fans devastated by the loss of a legend, and a London derby against West Ham.

Neill's first starting 11 suggested continuity with Nicholson. He restored three veterans in Mike England, Martin Peters and Cyril Knowles. Knowles was making his first appearance of the season.

When he entered the directors' box alongside Wale, Neill was greeted with a mixed response. While there were some cheers, there were at least as many boos and even some more colourful language from some unimpressed Spurs fans.

England got the first goal of the post-Nicholson era with a header when Knowles collected a short corner and floated in a cross. Chivers added the second with a header of his own from a Peters cross.

Chivers had battled gamely, coming out the better in an ongoing clash with West Ham's Tommy Taylor. He had hit the bar in the first half before scoring his goal. Taylor eventually required stitches on a gashed ankle suffered in one coming together with Spurs' number nine.

Knowles was booked, alongside West Ham's Billy Bonds, after the pair exchanged punches, but was also named man of the match.

The first match under a new manager for 16 years ended as a 2-1 win.

It was hardly the 10-4 victory of Nicholson's debut, but it was something. Frank Lampard was on target for the Hammers and Spurs' goalscorers were two players Neill would swiftly move on from – England and Chivers.

Neill once again outlined his difference of philosophy with Nicholson after the match, saying, 'It's all been a question of confidence and that is something nobody can give a team but themselves. I hope these two points will be the start of making them believe in themselves again.'

These were words that never could have come from the mouth of Nicholson – he would take responsibility upon himself – and once again hinted at the incompatibility that would eventually force a damaging rupture.

Despite the double blow to morale of Nicholson's departure and Neill's appointment, 27,959 fans were in attendance for the first match of the new era. It was comfortably their best gate of the season so far. The victory sent the Hammers to the bottom of the table and lifted Spurs up to 18th.

The biggest question in the press after the match was the future of Chivers. A move to Queens Park Rangers was mooted as an imminent possibility. Chivers himself told reporters to 'ask the boss' when questioned on his future.

The question was put directly to Neill, who said, 'Let's just say that for the moment he is too good of a player to let go.'

West Ham defender John McDowell said after the match that Chivers was – 'on that form' – England's finest forward. An unnamed Spurs player was somewhat more circumspect, quoted in the press as saying, 'Yes. great. Give him credit. But what about all the other weeks? Is he always going to play like that?'

Three days before the match, new England manager Don Revie – appointed to replace World Cup-winner Alf Ramsey after the failure to qualify for the 1974 tournament – had announced an 85-man[18] list of players called to a 'get together'. Revie explained that the purpose of the large squad

---

18 This was later revised down to 84 after it was discovered that John Robertson of Nottingham Forest was in fact born in Glasgow and dreamed not of playing for England, but of beating them.

was to demonstrate that 'nobody is really out of the reckoning'. Chivers had not been selected.

Next up, Spurs beat Wolverhampton Wanderers 3-2 with Chivers scoring twice and Peters adding another. Peters too would soon be sold by Neill. The recovery was short-lived, though, as Spurs lost their next three consecutive games, against Middlesbrough, Burnley and Chelsea.

The stuttering start under Neill continued but in mid-October things began to stabilise. Newly promoted Carlisle had been top of the league after three games but had begun to fall away, and Chivers scored as Spurs earned a point at home to the Cumbrians.

Three days later Arsenal – who had started their season as poorly as Spurs – visited White Hart Lane. After a tense opening 40 minutes, in which both sides looked largely as poor as their league form suggested, Martin Peters nodded a Knowles corner down for Perryman to hammer a half-volley past Arsenal keeper Jimmy Rimmer.

Perryman took a Liam Brady boot to the face in the second half – immediately developing a swelling that made him look more boxer than footballer – but played on and it was from his free kick that Peters again headed across goal, this time allowing Chivers to scramble home from close range. The 2-0 derby win took Tottenham out of the drop zone and left Arsenal bottom of the league.

Neill made his first signing shortly after that match. With Chivers and Conn suffering regular injuries, Neill prioritised the acquisition of a striker. Assistant Wilf Dixon was sent to scout in Scotland and discovered Dundee's John Duncan.

On a frozen and flooded pitch, Duncan had played in an unfamiliar midfield role as Dundee upset Jock Stein's mighty Celtic side 1-0 in the 1973 Scottish League Cup Final.[19]

---

19 The match was played with a line painted from sideline to sideline, all the way across the 18 yard box, as part of an offbeat trial to improve offside rulings. FIFA president Stanley Rous attended the match to observe.

The match had to be rescheduled for the early afternoon following the announcement of a national ban on generators which precluded the use of the floodlights at Hampden Park.

Duncan had 109 goals to his name, still the fifth highest in Dundee's history. He idolised Alan Gilzean, one of the few players to have scored more goals than him for Dundee. Alex Ferguson, who played and managed against Duncan, called him 'an exceptional striker'.

After his playing career was over, Duncan would be a success as a manager too. He led Chesterfield on a famous run to the FA Cup semi-finals in 1997, and also managed Ipswich Town and Scunthorpe United during his career.

Signing Duncan for £160,000 would prove a shrewd bargain. He lacked great speed, was unathletic and was not particularly graceful, but he knew how to score goals. Despite joining mid-season, he finished as Spurs' highest scorer with 20 goals in 37 appearances.

Duncan's particular prowess in aerial challenges and physical battles led him inevitably to injuries which would go some way to defining Tottenham's eventual fate.

Spurs had stabilised somewhat under Neill – they went eight games without defeat in October and November – but that form soon deserted them.

14

A wretched winter

THERE WAS virtually no snow, very little frost, and certainly no disruption to the football calendar in the winter of 1974/75. It was one of the mildest on record. Tottenham, though, endured a deep freeze, and would emerge blistered and nearly broken.

After a confident 3-0 win over Newcastle in early December, Spurs were 15th and closer in points to the top than the bottom of the table, but what momentum they had gathered since the arrival of their new manager soon began to fade. Then it disappeared completely.

First Ipswich Town smashed Spurs 4-0, then a week later John Duncan scored his fifth goal in ten games in a 2-1 defeat by Queens Park Rangers.

Back-to-back 1-1 draws against West Ham and Coventry steadied things somewhat before an FA Cup draw with Nottingham Forest.

Before the replay could take place, Forest took the hugely significant decision of appointing recently sacked Leeds United manager Brian Clough. Clough, sensationally dropping back down to the Second Division with Forest – he had worked in the Third Division with Brighton & Hove Albion before taking the Leeds job – got off to the perfect start by beating Tottenham 1-0.

Next up was a trip to St James' Park to face Newcastle, where Duncan scored again, but the day belonged to Alfie

Conn. Conn was making just his second league appearance since signing for the club months earlier – curiously the other had been a few weeks before, also against Newcastle – but he slipped easily into the team, opening the scoring at the end of a neat move that featured Duncan and Peters.

When the aptly named Willie McFaul tripped over himself and failed to stop a cross-cum-shot from Knowles, it was 2-0. Then Conn set Neighbour away down the wing, with Duncan's shot bouncing off McFaul and into the net for Spurs' third. Shortly before half-time, Conn struck again to give Tottenham a remarkable 4-0 half-time lead.

While Newcastle did reduce the deficit in the second period, Conn completed his hat-trick to seal a stunning 5-2 victory. Magpies manager Joe Harvey could only repeat after the match that could not believe what had happened.

In truth, Pat Jennings had been beaten at least five times but Knowles had made a handful of goal-line clearances, while Jennings himself had made a vital save in the first minute of the match.

The stunning victory over Newcastle was Tottenham's only win between 7 December and 28 March – a 111-day stretch.

It was also the 191st and final appearance for Ray Evans, who was sold to Millwall a few days later for £45,000. Evans had been at Spurs for nine years, joining as an apprentice before making his debut in 1969 against Arsenal.

Evans had missed just two league games and started both legs of the UEFA Cup Final the previous season, going close to creating an equaliser in Rotterdam from a free kick, but had lost his place to Phil Beal and slipped behind Joe Kinnear in the pecking order as well.

After being replaced during a home defeat to Stoke, captain Martin Peters left the stadium and went home, not even waiting for the match to finish. Neither the club nor the player addressed the issue publicly, but it was clear that Neill and Peters were not seeing eye-to-eye.

At the end of February, Neill told the *Daily Mirror* that relationships could yet be salvaged. He included Martin Chivers, saying, 'If they can prove that they can play again to their ability, there's no reason why they shouldn't stay.' Two days after the Stoke incident, Neill held a 'clear the air' session with his players.

Tottenham's fans had begun – if they had ever stopped – to loudly sing for Bill Nicholson to return and Neill to be removed, but their old manager was busy receiving an OBE at Buckingham Palace. The Queen Mother performed the investiture, with Nicholson being recognised for his services to football.

Chairman Sidney Wale was beginning to feel the pressure, too. Fans had begun to jeer him as much as the manager he had hired. As Spurs' misery continued, fans hoping for reinforcements were further disappointed when Wale gave a stark reminder of the club's financial situation. He said, 'I state categorically that we have no money available for transfers.'

The press reported that Spurs were losing £1,000 a week, and needed a crowd of at least 16,000 for every home match in order to break even – something that had only happened once so far during the season.

Mike England hosted a radio phone-in the next day and admitted, 'I don't think the club has been in such a desperate situation for a long time.'

A few days later, Neill took his team 1,000 miles to Belgrade for a friendly against Red Star. With Spurs having lost five of their last six league matches, their manager perhaps thought that a change of scenery would do them some good.

An unnamed player told the press while boarding the plane, 'The best place for us at the moment is out of the country.'

One player who did not make the trip was Martin Chivers, who was instead left in London to play for the reserves as they beat Birmingham City 2-1.

Chivers was not pleased, telling the *Daily Mirror*, 'I was the only member of the first-team squad not picked for the Belgrade trip who didn't hear it personally from the manager. Under both Bill Nicholson and Terry Neill, everyone seems to think I'm the problem. I can assure you that is not true. At least under Nicholson you knew where you stood.'

Chivers was watched by Chelsea at the match, and the newspapers were full of speculation that the England striker would move across London to join the Blues.

Tottenham won 1-0 in Belgrade courtesy of a goal from Chris Jones, but it didn't help them to rediscover their domestic form as they lost their next three matches, scoring just a single goal.

Neill was still in need of reinforcements and he acquired some in the shape of promising defender Don McAllister from Bolton for £80,000. McAllister would remain at Tottenham for six seasons as a near ever-present in the side.

McAllister signed as an aggressive 21-year-old with five years of experience under his belt, having been a regular in the Second and Third Divisions with the Trotters. Although not the most elegant of defenders, he was fearless and brought the aggression and physicality that Spurs would depend upon in the coming seasons. He was also quite capable with the ball at his feet, and would really find himself when Neill's successor – more committed to attacking football – took charge.

When Leicester – themselves a relegation-threatened side – hammered Spurs 3-0 in February, Neill was the subject of near-constant chanting from the Tottenham fans. Most of it was deemed 'x-certificate' and thus unprintable.

If Neill was feeling the pressure, he wasn't showing it. He admitted, 'If I was in their position, I'd probably be screaming the same things. If you can't take it, you have no right to be in the business.'

Leicester midfielder Alan Birchenall was scathing of Tottenham, saying, 'I know we've still got problems, but we don't have as many as Spurs. That's the worst Tottenham side I've ever seen.'

There were somewhat bizarre scenes after the match, when Neill seemed to be trying to cheer up the beat reporters. 'Don't look so worried,' Neill told them, 'it's not the end of the world.'

He was philosophical, and unflappable as ever, saying, 'My future is not in my hands. it's in the hands of my players. But I still have every confidence in my ability.'

Even the very real prospect of relegation couldn't dampen Neill's spirits, 'Even if we go down, we could come straight back up – then we would all be heroes.'

This was the perfect encapsulation of why – Arsenal connections aside – Tottenham fans would never warm to Neill. To them, the idea of Spurs going down was unthinkable, and a manager who could remain so even-keeled even in the stormiest of times was just not what they wanted.

On 1 March Tottenham travelled to Derby County. The man standing opposite Neill in the Derby dugout was Dave Mackay, who had returned to the Baseball Ground as manager in 1973 and was on the way to winning the First Division title.

Mackay's side beat Spurs 3-1, with future Arsenal boss Bruce Rioch scoring one of the goals. In the aftermath Neill again admitted that his side were facing relegation, and refused to place any blame on his predecessor or the club, 'I inherited no problems – that would just be making excuses. There's no denying it's a desperate situation and I accept criticism and a large share of the responsibility.'

A week later, Neill finally quit his post as Northern Ireland manager to focus on the job of saving Tottenham from relegation.

With that desperate fight against the drop now the sole focus of his mind, Neill made perhaps his biggest decision yet when Martin Peters was sold to Norwich.

Peters would go on to make over 200 league appearances for the Canaries and, after doing so at West Ham and Spurs, became a legend at a third club. His signing was described by John Bond, Norwich's manager at the time, as 'the greatest thing that ever happened to Norwich City Football Club'.

Peters' departure was something of a shock. Having captained England just a year before, he left Spurs for just £50,000. Neill explained his decision, simply saying that he had refused to sit in the stands when named as a reserve for a match against Stoke. Neill's memory does not quite match up with reality, as Peters started both games against Stoke that season, but there was certainly a clash of personalities.

Chivers adds some revealing colour to the evident lack of rapport between manager and captain. According to the ex-England striker, Peters told Neill that he could manage Tottenham better and the head coach responded that Peters could leave if he felt that way.

Neill was quite critical of his outgoing captain, saying, 'In spite of Peters' ability. I could not dismiss what he had said and I was left with no option but to sell him. He had been the club captain yet he has done less than most during the present situation.'

Phil Beal was reported as being close to following Peters out the door, with Spurs asking just £10,000 for his signature. Crystal Palace were the reported favourites but he ended up staying until the end of the season, when he joined Brighton on a free transfer.

Perryman was named captain after Peters' departure.

After a home defeat to Liverpool two weeks later, four points separated Spurs from safety. Suddenly they found their best form of the season and reeled off victories against QPR, Wolves, and relegation rivals Luton Town. John Duncan scored in each win.

In the third of those matches, Alfie Conn scored the winner in a scrappy game. Afterwards, Neill virtually apologised for Spurs winning, saying, 'I can't feel embarrassed because we desperately need the points, but I do feel terribly sorry for Luton.'

Duncan scored for a fourth match running but Spurs' streak ended with Burnley winning by the odd goal in five.

That defeat set the table for a huge London derby.

15

Salvation or damnation

TELEVISION COVERAGE of the match dubbed it 'the most important in the history of the two clubs'. Chelsea were 17th and one point ahead of Spurs before the match but with a vastly inferior goal difference. Victory for the Blues would all but save them from the drop with only two matches left to play. Spurs sat 18th but had won three of their last four matches.

Joe Kinnear and Jimmy Neighbour – both veterans of the Bill Nicholson era – had missed Spurs' previous game through illness but returned to face Chelsea, as did Martin Chivers on the bench.

A crowd of 51,000 packed out White Hart Lane and thousands were turned away as the gates were closed before kick-off. A dozen or so fans even climbed the television broadcast tower to watch.

Kick-off was delayed by three minutes because of a pre-match pitch invasion. The FA later launched an investigation and Spurs would not be finally free of the threat of a potential fine or points deduction until the following June.

Once the match belatedly got underway, Chelsea started well and Spurs looked nervous. The Blues had a penalty shout almost from kick-off and Pat Jennings was forced to make a strong save minutes later.

A young Ray Wilkins – Chelsea's captain on the day – was driving waves of attacks forward as Spurs' moves continued to come apart on the boggy pitch.

Jennings made another diving save, denying a close-range header from forward Ian Hutchinson. At half-time it was goalless and Spurs very much had Jennings to thank. His brilliance had become routine in his ten years as Tottenham's number one, so much so that another remarkable performance against Chelsea barely drew comment.

In the second half, Steve Perryman picked up a loose ball and played it down the left for John Duncan who skipped one challenge and rode another before whipping it across goal. The pass found Chris Jones who turned and rolled the ball into the path of Perryman who fired past John Phillips in the Chelsea goal.

Chelsea still only needed to score once and – after a wild scramble in the Spurs goal – they finally forced the ball over the line, but it was disallowed for a handball. Even Jennings had made an uncharacteristic flap at the ball in the build-up.

As if sparked by coming so close to the goal they needed, Chelsea came forward again in search of the equaliser. Jennings made a commanding leap for a high ball but it slipped out of his giant hands and the ball fell to Wilkins who inexplicably fired wide.

A rare Spurs foray forward yielded a corner and the initial Chelsea clearance fell to Alfie Conn on the edge of the box. The Scot ripped a powerful low shot with his left foot past Phillips and Spurs had a 2-0 lead.

Conn had emerged as a rare bright spot for Tottenham fans. Already known as 'The King of White Hart Lane' among supporters and immortalised by a piece of graffiti which read 'Alfie Conn is god', his individual flair was meaningful in a difficult season.

Chelsea struggled on but Tottenham held out until the final whistle. When that whistle blew, Spurs had leapfrogged their cross-London rivals and moved out of the drop zone at their expense.

The Blues would not escape relegation and would go on to bounce up and down between the First and Second Divisions until finally being promoted for good in 1989.

The match against Chelsea was another marked by serious outbreaks of violence in the crowd. Scores of fans spilled on to the pitch in running battles that led the evening news. The image of supporters attacking a police officer, printed in newspapers the following day, became a symbol of the ongoing issue of violence at football matches. It was often reprinted to accompany editorials decrying the scourge of hooliganism.

Despite their vital victory over Chelsea, Spurs were still not yet safe and two fixtures remained – Arsenal at Highbury followed Leeds at home on the final day.

On 26 April 1975 Tottenham crossed north London to face the Gunners and sat 19th, good enough for safety in a 22-team league.

Arsenal were on something of a journey of rediscovery themselves. Following their Double win in 1971, they had lost the following year's FA Cup Final to Leeds and were in the midst of a 16-year trophy drought.

They were just three points ahead of Spurs, and not a particularly strong team at Highbury. They had won just nine home games that season, and nine the season before.

Spurs had won the corresponding fixture the previous season with a lone goal from Chris McGrath. Martin Chivers and Steve Perryman had scored the goals as they'd beaten Arsenal in the reverse fixture in October, too.

Arsenal's goalkeeper Jimmy Rimmer broke his finger in training before the match, and was forced to sit out. His back-up Jeff Barnett made his first league appearance since December 1972, and his first in any competition in over two years. Midfielder Eddie Bailey – a staple of their Double-winning side – was also missing. Spurs, meanwhile, were able to name the same 11 which had beaten Chelsea the previous Saturday.

Tottenham were in trouble early though and only the desperate lunge of Cyril Knowles stopped Brian Kidd's goal-bound shot crossing the line.

But Arsenal kept coming. Cutting back on to his left foot out on the right, Liam Brady chipped a dangerous pass into the box. Kidd took off once again and got in behind Keith Osgood, who managed to get a touch on the ball but couldn't clear. Jennings dived, missed, and Arsenal were ahead.

When Barnett mishandled a floated Knowles free kick, Conn tried to toe-poke an equaliser but defender Sammy Nelson cleared off the line.

In the second half, a tidy run from Terry Naylor gave Perryman the chance to charge into the box. Barnett smothered the chance but the ball squeezed out and sat up invitingly – almost on the penalty spot – for Conn. The Scot arrived at full sprint and placed his low shot inches wide of the post. Conn fell to the pitch, his head in his hands.

As the Spurs players walked off at full time, Conn was still shaking his head. Perryman jogged to catch him and gave him an encouraging slap on the back.

Anything but defeat against Arsenal would have made Spurs safe from relegation, but while they were losing at Highbury, Luton and Chelsea had both drawn their final league fixtures, leaving the Lilywhites second from bottom.

It wasn't over yet because Tottenham had a game in hand. Unfortunately for them, that game was against Leeds United who would face Bayern Munich in the European Cup Final a month later in Paris.

The night before facing Leeds, Terry Neill brought hypnotist and clairvoyant Romark – real name Ronald Markham – to the hotel.

Martin Chivers, fit but not selected against Arsenal, had been told by Neill the previous week that he could leave in the summer, regardless of whether Spurs stayed up. Neill took Chivers into a room and introduced him to Romark who explained that he had foreseen the next day's newspaper headlines, 'Chivers Back With a Goal'. Chivers was laughing on the inside but kept quiet.

Next the hypnotist had the players visualise their greatest moments. Jennings joked that some of them would have struggled to think of anything. Afterwards, they had champagne and cake to celebrate Chivers' 30th birthday the day before.

Monday, 28 April dawned cool but swiftly began to heat up. As kick-off approached the temperature rose towards 70ºC. It would be the warmest day of the year so far.

Before the match, the directors were shaking with fear. One took a heart tablet. Another's saucer rattled as he drank a cup of tea. Spurs' finances, already stretched by several lean, Europe-free seasons, would be strained further by relegation.

Just two days had passed since the defeat at Highbury, but with most clubs having completed their fixtures all eyes were on White Hart Lane.

At least the ground was full. The biggest crowd of the season, 49,886, packed the stadium for what could be Spurs' last game as a First Division side.

The match had barely got going before Conn was fouled on the edge of the area. Cyril Knowles stepped up and fired a brilliant free kick beyond David Stewart in the Leeds goal.

A clever move from a second-half free kick enabled Chivers to double Spurs' lead, before Knowles converted a penalty won by Perryman to make it 3-0.

Future Tottenham first-team coach Joe Jordan pulled one back, before Conn dashed through the Leeds defence to score a decisive fourth.

Peter Lorimer scored late to make it 4-2 but Conn – who had been involved in all four of Spurs' goals – took the ball to the corner flag and even sat on it to ensure Leeds would not complete an unlikely comeback.

Conn had exorcised the demons of the derby miss, Tottenham were safe, and Chivers was back with a goal.

After scoring in four of the final seven matches, Perryman had shone again against Leeds, while the home fans chanted Bill Nicholson's name after the full time whistle.

The crowd refused to go home until Neill came out to see them. They were chanting his name as they had Nicholson's. A policeman entered the Spurs dressing room to ask Neill whether he would do as they demanded. Reflecting on nine months of criticism and no small share of abuse from many supporters, Neill said the fans could 'go and get stuffed'.

Celebrations spilled out of White Hart Lane on to Tottenham High Road. As the singing, dancing crowd passed a hospital, police intervened and attempted to quieten them.

After the scuffle that followed, six members of the crowd were charged with various offences including the use of insulting language and refusing instruction from a police officer. Five received fines of £245 and the other was remanded in custody.

Tottenham had survived their most difficult season in 40 years, but there were still deep problems running through the club. Neill had slashed away at the ageing squad left to him by Nicholson but had not yet succeeded in adding much fresh talent in return.

The acquisition of John Duncan had probably saved Spurs, but the future of fellow striker Martin Chivers hung over things. Tottenham finished the season with a younger, less experienced, and probably less talented team than the group with which they had begun it.

The collapse of crowd numbers was also significant. From the highs of the Double-winning season – when Spurs were the best-attended team in the country and well over one million fans went through the turnstiles at White Hart Lane – attendances had collapsed in the near-relegation season.

Just 556,165 fans – almost exactly half the number of 1960/61 – attended league matches at White Hart Lane in 1974/75. There were no European matches or cup runs to pad out the bottom line, either.

While television ownership, which had increased from 67 per cent to essentially 100 per cent – in British households in the previous 15 years, was a contributory factor, that does not explain the trend. The total number of fans attending matches across the British top flight had actually risen slightly over the previous decade.

League champions Derby County, Stoke City and Birmingham City were among the 12 clubs with better attendance than Spurs.

Fans were put off by the nature of Nicholson's departure, the misery of watching their team lose, and the style of football the team were now playing.

Where Nicholson was a football aesthete, Neill was far more pragmatic. He was willing to play defensively. Nicholson insisted on attacking teams with flying wingers and numbers in attack, while Neill put numbers in midfield and insisted on caution.

Many supporters remember this aspect of the revolution at their club that season as being worse than watching their team lose.

Those supporters had had precious little to cheer in that season, both on and off the pitch. Not only had they watched their team disintegrate in record time but the British economy was dissolving at a similar rate. Inflation, already at historic levels, reached a high of 25 per cent that year. Two general elections were held in the same year for the first time since 1910.

As Dominic Sandbook writes in his history of Britain in the 1970s, working-class culture – of which football had always been a part – was dying a swift death in the early part of the decade. Economic, political, and social turmoil were eating away at it.

The *Observer Magazine* described working-class life as having become 'squalid and grim'. By the middle of the decade, a flurry of books with downcast, depressing titles described the collapse of British glory, the end of empire, and the decline of a once great nation.

There is a degree of hyperbole in all of this, but it does reflect a genuine notion that things had gone badly wrong.

Violence within football grounds, and the aggressive response to it from authorities, helped to make them less inviting places to be. Lower crowds meant lower gates and, subsequently, less money to spend on upgrades and even repairs.

Tottenham fared better than most clubs in this sense. There were money troubles to come, but White Hart Lane never threatened to become a crumbling ruin like some other formerly great British grounds.

Part 3: False Dawn, and Demise

16

The rebuild that never was

TERRY NEILL had saved Spurs. If he had not quite performed a miracle, it was probably the next best thing. Tottenham's start to the season, just four points from eight games,[20] had been historically bad, and five wins from their final seven was a remarkable turnaround.

The new manager had also begun a long overdue overhaul of the team. Neill's approach had not been gentle. In his first eight months in charge, Ray Evans, Phil Holder, Joe Kinnear, Mike Dillon and Martin Peters were all sold.

With over 880 combined games for Spurs represented among the outgoing players, Neill had taken a huge gamble. The quintet had accounted for 133 appearances in the previous season alone.

To make things worse, Mike England had retired. Though he had played 33 games the previous season, and 397 since joining the club, he had been suffering persistent ankle issues. But the giant Welshman soon came out of retirement, joining Cardiff City where he helped them to gain promotion from the Third Division. England then moved to the United States, joining Seattle Sounders as captain.

Neill blamed England for his departure, saying he had 'walked out on the club in the middle of a relegation battle'.

---

20 Spurs would famously have a worse start in the 2007/08 season, taking two points from eight games under Spanish coach Juande Ramos.

England had never been a particular fan of Neill's either, though he had actually scored in the manager's first game in charge.

Holder moved to Crystal Palace before he too ended up in the North American Soccer League with Memphis Rogues, and Kinnear later retired after a season with Brighton & Hove Albion.

While Don McAllister and John Duncan had been signed and contributed to Spurs' great escape, Neill knew he needed to add more talent. He now faced a new challenge. Having kept Tottenham up, he had to rebuild the team to avoid a repeat the next year.

Spurs announced that they had raised £500,000 by taking out a loan against property they owned. The intention was to vault the club away from danger. That injection of funds put them in a rare position as many clubs were struggling financially. The recession which had dragged through the last two years was technically now over, but inflation remained shockingly high – above 25 per cent – and debts taken on to survive the hard times were now coming due.

Many clubs were unable to spend. Liverpool would make only two signings in 1975/76, Arsenal would add just one player, and Leeds, having just made it all the way to the European Cup Final, didn't sign anyone at all.

Spurs needed serious reinforcements and set about trying to recruit some big hitters.

Second Division side Sunderland had pulled off a shock upset against the mighty Leeds United in the 1973 FA Cup Final. Ian Porterfield scored the winning goal, denying Don Revie a second FA Cup in as many years. It also turned out to be Revie's last cup final as Leeds boss, although he would win the league title again the next year.

None of Sunderland's XI were full internationals, vanishingly rare in the history of FA Cup, but centre-back Dave Watson made his England debut the following season.

By May 1975 Watson had won 12 caps and would win over 50 more, as Neill identified the star as an ideal addition to his side. Billy Hughes – the Scottish striker who had taken the corner that resulted in Sunderland's winner at Wembley – was also targeted.

As good a judge of talent as Revie had also tried to sign Hughes and described him as, 'One of the most exciting players I've seen. He loves to go forward. He runs straight at opponents forcing them to commit themselves and can shoot with either foot.'

Strike power and defensive reinforcements were two areas of dire need for Neill's Tottenham and they moved quickly.

Watson had lodged an official transfer request, alerting Spurs. Hughes too had been made available after Sunderland failed to gain promotion in 1974/75.

Tottenham were far from the only club interested; Liverpool and Arsenal were also considered leading contenders to sign the 28-year-old. The fee was expected to be a world record for a defender, in excess of the £267,000 Genoa paid for Milan legend Roberto Rosato. Tottenham's offer for the duo was to be £300,000 plus Ralph Coates.

Born in Nottingham, Watson preferred a move to the Midlands and was not keen on London. Manchester City convinced him to join them instead for £275,000, plus young defender Jeff Clarke.

Hughes didn't leave at all that summer, remaining at Sunderland until 1977.

Having failed to land either of the Sunderland duo, Neill switched his attention to out-of-favour Arsenal star Charlie George.

Arsenal had a squad in comparable need of repair, meaning they were a competitor for Spurs in the transfer market, but they had to sell to buy. This meant George was available. Veteran captain Alan Ball was also put up for sale.

George had been a scorer of important goals for the Gunners, chipping in with five in the run-in to the 1971 league title and four more in the FA Cup that season.

He had missed most of 1974/75 with an ankle injury, but was still just 24 and had the potential to form a well-balanced midfield at Tottenham.

Alongside Alfie Conn and Steve Perryman, Tottenham would have penetrative passing, skilful dribbling and determined tackling.

In 1974 George's value had been estimated at almost £300,000 but Arsenal's economic need and his injury issues meant a bargain was in the offing. A fee was agreed – between £100,000 and £125,000 – and George even passed his medical but changed his mind at the last minute. Given that George had officially requested to leave Arsenal, he was not legally entitled to the standard share of the transfer fee. Nevertheless, he wanted his cut.

League champions Derby County matched Tottenham's offer and included a five per cent share for George. Neill, believing the deal already agreed, refused to match Derby's offer. George signed for Dave Mackay's Derby and enjoyed an excellent season, scoring a hat-trick in the European Cup against Real Madrid before eventually being sold to Southampton for £350,000.

Chairman Sidney Wale told the *Daily Mirror*, 'I'm extremely disappointed that this transfer has fallen through. We had done all the spade work. George had been given a thorough medical. We were expecting him to sign.'

Wale said that they were considering lodging an official complaint but Mackay denied any wrongdoing, saying, 'All was done fair and square.' He insisted that any inquiry would cause him 'no embarrassment'.

Still looking for experience and leadership, Neill turned to Liverpool's Ray Kennedy and Luton Town midfielder Peter Anderson but failed with moves for both. He even tried to sign Arsenal veteran Ball, who chose Second Division Southampton instead.

During the close season, Newcastle United sacked manager Joe Harvey and his coaching staff, including 40-year-old former Workington and Scunthorpe defender Keith Burkinshaw.

Burkinshaw had begun his career in the Liverpool reserve team, playing under trainer Bob Paisley. While Paisley later admitted that his former player was not quite of First Division playing standard, he said that Burkinshaw 'was a very sensible and professional lad'.

The three-time European Cup winner was unsurprised by Burkinshaw's later success, emphasising his first-class approach to football, and the deep thought he gave to it. Burkinshaw made a playing career at Workington and was eventually made manager of the Cumbrian side, but quit when the chairman insisted upon carte blanche in regards to team selections.

Burkinshaw rounded out his playing days at Scunthorpe, briefly taking over as manager, before being hired as a coach at Newcastle. He was a very popular man on Tyneside. When the Magpies had won the Anglo-Italian Cup, the manager and players had received bonuses. However, Burkinshaw was left out. Such was their affection for their coach, the players pooled their money and shared it with him.

Among other roles, Burkinshaw ran infamous pre-season workouts at Newcastle, where the players accepted him as a 'hard, but fair' coach. When he was sacked, they got together to buy him a gold watch.

Neill, who seemed to have a knack for quickly picking up news, heard that Burkinshaw was suddenly available. He phoned the Yorkshireman and offered him a job.

Although it did not seem like it at the time, that was a significant phone call. Burkinshaw would go on to win more trophies as Spurs manager than anyone not called Bill Nicholson.

Burkinshaw was a rising star as a coach. He had also been offered Birmingham City's youth development program but preferred the allure of First Division Tottenham, saying, 'Spurs are a big club with traditions to revive.'

Before finalising his move to White Hart Lane, Burkinshaw had to complete a coaching course at Lilleshall. He took the course alongside Bobby Robson.

Peter Shreeves was also brought in as a specialist youth coach. Neill already recognised that Spurs had a crop of exciting youngsters who would require careful coaching – chief among them was 17-year-old Glenn Hoddle.

Shreeves had been coaching part-time at Arsenal but had not been offered a full-time job, and had passed The Knowledge to become a London cab driver in case his football career stalled.

One victim of Neill's reorganisation of the club was chief scout Charlie Faulkner. Faulkner had been at the club since 1968 and counted Steve Perryman, Chris McGrath, Chris Jones, Terry Naylor, Keith Osgood, Graham Souness and Glenn Hoddle among players he had recruited. He was also the final member of Nicholson's backroom staff still at the club.

Another notable development that summer was UEFA's decision to ban Leeds from European competition for two years. Following the riots in Paris before and after their European Cup Final defeat in May, European football's governing body set a steep precedent with their punishment and in 1985, following the Heysel disaster – in which 39 people died as a result of violence before the European Cup Final between Liverpool and Juventus – all English clubs were handed an indeterminate ban from European football, later reduced to five years.

17

A solid season

TOTTENHAM HAD failed to find the reinforcements that they so clearly needed, and Terry Neill faced another issue in the form of Alfie Conn. Conn, whose individual skill had provided rare moments for Spurs fans to cheer during the previous difficult season, had asked for a pay rise. When no new contract was forthcoming, the Scottish midfielder handed in a written transfer request.

Next, Ralph Coates joined the list of Neill's problems. Coates, whose contract had expired, was keen to stay but was only offered the same terms on which he had signed in 1971. With the massive inflation which had wracked the British economy in the intervening years, Tottenham had effectively offered Coates a 49 per cent pay cut. Coates was furious, lashing out in the press and labelling the club 'unfair'.

Neill's first pre-season began with a rather unimpressive tour of Germany. First came a 1-1 draw against East German side Rot-Weiss Essen. Next was a 2-1 defeat at the hands of Karlsruhe. Another 1-1 draw followed, this time against Hannover, although Spurs got their first win of the pre-season schedule in August when Jones – who had scored against Essen and Hannover – got the only goal to beat NAC Breda.

Martin Chivers wrote later that this tour underlined Neill's limitations as a coach. 'No skills, no coaching, no tactics: just running until we dropped,' was Chivers' summary.

Jones scored again in the final match of pre-season, a 4-1 hammering of Bristol Rovers. Chivers got a brace and Coates added another from long range.

Despite the £500,000 raised for new signings, Spurs hadn't made a single one. Even in the week before the season began Neill made a £150,000 offer for Carlisle defender Bill Green, he offered Conn in exchange for Birmingham's Kenny Burns, and he enquired about Coventry winger Tommy Hutchinson. But none joined.

Neill was frustrated. He felt that the club's board were content with survival and lacked the ambition to push for the titles he thought they could win. In the context of the money raised to back him in the transfer market, this is a difficult argument to accept, but either way the manager was not happy. Ultimately the fallout would not truly be felt until the following summer.

One positive note was the withdrawal of Conn's transfer request. The Scot was moved by reports of Tottenham being 'inundated with calls for me to stay. If there's any way I can repay that loyalty, I'm ready to do so. If [the club] make a decent offer, I'll jump at the chance to stay'.

The new campaign opened against Middlesbrough. They had won the Second Division in 1974 and finished seventh the following season while having good runs in the League Cup and Texaco Cup.

Eight of Tottenham's starting 11 had also been in the team against Leeds on the final day of 1974/75. Two of the three brought in – Neil McNab, Jimmy Neighbour – were both already at the club before Neill even arrived.

There was little optimism on the terraces after the previous season's great escape, the summer of failed transfer bids, and the underwhelming pre-season performances.

Chris Jones volleyed the ball into the net from an Osgood cross early on against Boro but his goal was disallowed for offside. Steve Perryman scored the winner in what would be

Joe Kinnear's final match for the club before joining Brighton. It was Tottenham's first opening-day win since 1972.

Next up were Ipswich Town, who had been something of a bogey team for Spurs since the early 1960s, but with injury and illness reducing their strength Tottenham looked a good chance to get a second straight win.

In fact, they came within an inch of losing. A deflected shot from long range gave Ipswich the lead. The linesman raised his flag only to lower it, and this sparked Terry Naylor – a defender so passionate he had not one but two evocative nicknames ('nutter' and 'meathook') – to protest with such vehemence that he was booked. To earn a caution in the 1970s without having physically done anything was quite an achievement.

John Duncan was thrown on as a substitute for Naylor, and within five minutes he had Spurs level. The Scot leapt highest and headed home a Jimmy Neighbour free kick. But then, in the final moments, Ipswich keeper Paul Cooper hoofed the ball downfield to Terry Austin who flicked it on to Roger Osborne. Osborne smashed his shot beyond Pat Jennings and turned to celebrate a late, late win, only to see the linesman with his flag once again raised. This time the flag remained in the air and the goal was ruled out with Cooper deemed to have carried the ball out of his area before punting it.

Ipswich manager Bobby Robson was furious, insisting that even if Cooper was out of his box, 'It couldn't have been more than an inch.'

Three days after Ipswich came a trip to Anfield. Liverpool were on their way to a First Division and UEFA Cup double that season, and had no reason to fear Tottenham.

Despite the apparent difference in quality, Spurs built their attacks with confidence, creating opportunities for Jones, Chivers, and John Pratt.

Then Conn went on a 50-yard run that Liverpool could only halt by fouling him. Cyril Knowles crossed from the left and Duncan – always able to sniff out a chance – found the ball in the box and put Spurs ahead.

On 40 minutes, Jones ran on to a long pass from McAllister and rounded Ray Clemence in the Liverpool goal to make it 2-0. A shock upset, and Tottenham's first win at Anfield since 1911, seemed to be on the cards.

But the second half was a demonstration of why Liverpool would go on to be champions. Kevin Keegan dragged the Reds back into the match with a penalty before two goals in two minutes from Jimmy Case and Steve Heighway gave them a 3-2 win.

Case's goal was particularly galling for Spurs. He so badly mishit his shot that Jennings's dive saw him hit the ground too quickly, from where he could only watch the ball roll in.

Liverpool manager Bob Paisley said afterwards that too many more games like that would 'give somebody a thrombosis'.

Neill was 'very disappointed' with the result but spoke with the confidence of a manager who really believed that he was building something, 'I thought we could have slaughtered them, but we were still 30-40 per cent below our true potential in that first half.'

Mike Dillon, an occasional first-team player over the previous few seasons, was sold to Pelé's New York Cosmos, becoming perhaps the first British player sold to an American club for a transfer fee.

Despite encouraging performances, Spurs were tenth and next they faced a trip to face a rising force in British football, West Ham United.

John Lyall had succeeded long-term Hammers boss Ron Greenwood in 1974, winning the FA Cup in his first year by beating Fulham 2-0 in the Wembley final. In 1975/76 he had his eyes on the league title, as well as success in the domestic cups and UEFA Cup Winners' Cup. His team would certainly test Neill's again.

Once more Tottenham fought hard and created chances, but fortune deserted them at Upton Park. Jennings came for a second-half cross and missed the ball completely, leaving his goal open for Keith Robson to head home the only goal of the match. The win took West Ham top, and left Spurs 13th.

Neill refused to blame Jennings, instead simply saying, 'This must be his first mistake in ten years. It's just a shame it came when it did.'

With Spurs struggling for a spark, journalist Harry Harris called Neill, suggesting that the academy prodigy Hoddle be given a chance. He said Neill had no idea who Hoddle was, but the youngster made his debut against Norwich the next week.

Chivers had been dropped, while Conn, Coates and Perryman were all injured. Tottenham had three 17-year-olds in the starting line-up, and Hoddle on the bench.

In fact, with 18-year-old right-back Ian Smith also making his debut alongside the slightly more experienced 19-year-olds Osgood and Jones, Spurs' XI against Norwich was among their youngest of all time.

Just 18 minutes in Knowles limped off and Hoddle came on in his place, wearing the number 12 shirt.

The versatile John Pratt dropped into left-back, allowing Hoddle to play through the middle. Pratt had been working with Tottenham's youth teams and had actually coached Hoddle. His presence certainly helped the youngster.

Moments into his debut, Hoddle, 'high on adrenaline', won a header against Norwich centre-back Duncan Forbes, accidentally elbowing him in the process. Forbes landed on his back, blood flowing from his nose.

Forbes was known as a hard defender, even by the standards of the 1970s. He worked on building sites every summer. Former team-mate Dave Stringer said of Forbes that 'if he shouted in Norwich it could be heard in Yarmouth', some 20 miles away.

A man of granite, so tough that he once pretended to rob a Barclays Bank just for a laugh, Forbes lived for the individual duel of man-marking the opposition's best forward. He was hospitalised many times and suffered at least eight broken noses during his playing career. In short, Forbes was the last player that the skinny, teenaged Hoddle would be expected to send flying.

As Hoddle tried to apologise, Chivers came up and warned him to steer well clear of Forbes for the rest of the match. Hoddle followed the advice.

Pratt gave Tottenham the lead with a long-range goal before a deflected shot brought Norwich level. With half an hour to play, Neighbour crossed to Duncan who controlled the ball with one foot and scored with the other to restore Spurs' lead but in the 80th minute Norwich got their equaliser and the match finished 2-2.

Hoddle came close to marking his debut with a brilliant goal. He flicked the ball over an onrushing defender and volleyed it but missed the target. It was a sign of things to come.

In the space of those first 72 minutes on a senior football pitch, Hoddle went from feeling claustrophobic to feeling completely at home. Years later, Hoddle remembered moments of that first taste of First Division football. The size of the crowd made the pitch 'feel smaller'. Chivers recounted that Hoddle had told him he couldn't believe how well the former England striker could head the ball to his feet in midfield, even under pressure from defenders. He remembered too that Hoddle 'played well' and passed 'nicely' in the match, receiving applause for touches of skill.

Neill insisted that he had selected Hoddle, as well as Smith, 'because they're good players', but admitted that 'the economic state of the game dictates that these youngsters have got to be what our future is all about'.

Arsenal and Chelsea also suddenly saw their teams filled with teenagers as the British economic recovery continued to drag.

Hoddle continued to train with the first team thereafter, but would have to wait for his next chance to start.

In the aftermath, it emerged that Knowles had badly pulled his hamstring and would miss at least the next month of football.

Two days after the Norwich match the lead headline on the front page of the *Daily Mirror* was 'Madmen!' This came with a report on the shocking violence connected with football over the previous weekend. Over 150 fans had been arrested and two trains ransacked, one burned and a fourth looted of mailbags. Three people were stabbed and scores of others injured.

The worst incidents occurred at Luton Town v Chelsea where visiting fans caused the match to be halted by invading the pitch. Players traded punches with the supporters, two policemen were set upon and at least 350 people were thrown out of the ground. The violence simply continued outside, with shops and cars having windows smashed. Even a police car was destroyed.

Coach drivers had refused to even take Spurs fans to Carrow Road, fearing the inevitable destruction to their vehicles.

On the same day, 97 were arrested, 77 were injured and three stabbed at the Old Firm derby between Rangers and Celtic.

These reports were becoming a regular fixture of weekend football coverage. One new wrinkle was the apparent addition of 'kung-fu style throwing stars' to the arsenal of those involved.

Central defender William 'Big Willie' Young joined Tottenham for around £100,000 from Aberdeen in September. The 6ft 3in Young – who worked on oil rigs during the summer while playing in Scotland – had a wild streak. Earlier that season he had been banned for life from playing for Scotland after 'an incident' in a Copenhagen nightclub.

The trouble was supposedly sparked over a disputed bill at the Bonaparte nightclub. Five Scotland players were removed from the club after police were called. Young himself claimed that it was simply 'a misunderstanding'.

He had only been available for Spurs because he had stormed out of an Aberdeen match – kicking a hole in the dressing room door – leading the Scottish club to listen to offers.

Young was big, strong, and slow. His time at Tottenham was short but he proved useful in the development of young Keith Osgood. Osgood, the more elegant footballer, could play wider and focus on bringing the ball out, leaving the physical game to Young.

Young would only stay for two seasons, eventually crossing the north London divide for a longer, more successful stint at Arsenal.

Spurs had faced Norwich with nine first-team players missing due to injury, but some finally began to return ahead of the next match, a trip to Manchester United.

Despite the improving situation, Neill's 14-man squad contained five teenagers. The combination of Neill's attempt to reshape the squad, economic realities and a prodigious crop of talented youngsters meant that this situation was not as disastrous as it might have been.

The trip to Old Trafford marked the first anniversary of Neill taking charge at Tottenham. The preceding 12 months had not been short on upheaval, and the difference between the line-ups in his first match and the United clash was telling. Ray Evans, Phil Beal, Mike England, Cyril Knowles, Ralph Coates, Martin Peters, Martin Chivers were all gone. Evans, England, Peters and Beal had already been sold. None of the others would ever be Tottenham first-team players again.

United, relegated in 1974, had been promoted as Second Division champions in 1975 and were building towards their first real successes of the post-Matt Busby era. They were unbeaten and top of the league, having won five of their first six games so the trip represented Spurs' biggest test of the season. After good performances which had not really been reflected in the results, this would indicate where Neill's team really stood.

Hoddle, whose name was erroneously reported as 'Phil Hoddle', was left out as Perryman and Duncan came back into the side. Ian Smith kept his place too but that was his last appearance, joining Rotherham United the following summer. It would not be a match to remember for the young full-back.

Chris Jones gave Spurs a surprise lead after just five minutes but United responded with a long spell of pressure; six corners in four minutes saw Tottenham defending desperately. Though they survived that, as well as a rogue announcement over the tannoy that bombs had been hidden around the ground, United continued to press. The hosts' equaliser, when it did come, featured more than a touch of fortune as in the 26th minute Smith attempted a clearance, only to see it deflect off Pratt and shoot past Pat Jennings. Then, just before half-time, Smith gave away a penalty and United took a 2-1 lead into the break.

Right after the teams came back out United extended their lead. Jimmy Neighbour then won a penalty of his own but could only find the crossbar. With eight minutes remaining, Jennings's long ball found Jones who headed on to Chivers. The veteran striker scored for 3-2 but Spurs couldn't find an equaliser.

The match at Old Trafford showed that Spurs had certain qualities but were still lacking in other areas. United, who would go on to finish just four points off the top and qualify for the UEFA Cup, were a far better team but Tottenham had pushed them.

Three days later, Jones scored again as Spurs beat Fourth Division side Watford 1-0 in the League Cup at Vicarage Road.

A happy moment: Martin Chivers and Bill Nicholson share a smile after the 1971 League Cup victory.

Spurs scoop the world: Keith Burkinshaw poses with new signings Ricardo Villa and Osvaldo Ardiles, in July 1978.

The icing on the cake: Garth Crooks and Steve Archibald took Tottenham to the next level in 1980/81.

Cockney Cup winners: Dave Mackay holds the FA Cup aloft after victory over Chelsea at Wembley in 1967.

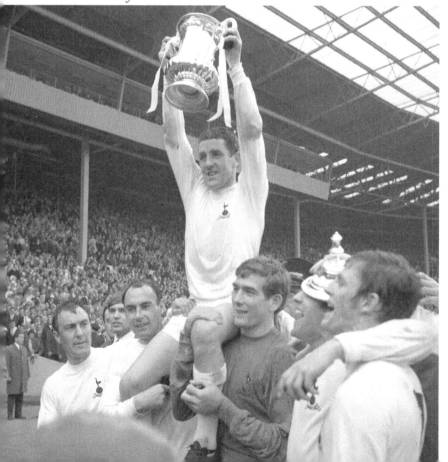

The happy warrior: Steve Perryman was one of the few Tottenham players to enjoy his time under Terry Neill.

The dynamic duo: Bill Nicholson played a vital role in Keith Burkinshaw taking Tottenham back to the top.

So near, and yet ... Dave Mackay's header cannons off the crossbar during the 1962 European Cup semi-final second leg at White Hart Lane.

The only way is up: Tottenham fans react to relegation in 1977 with optimism.

The great escape: Spurs fans flood the pitch at White Hart Lane after their team relegate Chelsea and give themselves a lifeline.

Earning his spurs: Glenn Hoddle celebrates scoring against Crystal Palace during Tottenham's successful promotion campaign in 1977.

History made: Bill Nicholson congratulates his players on completing the Double, after telling them they hadn't been at their best.

An unsung hero: John Duncan's goals fired Tottenham to promotion in 1977/78, and his absence probably sent them down the year before.

266 and out: Jimmy Greaves left an indelible mark on Tottenham's history, even if he left the club too soon.

Next up was the visit of reigning champions Derby County, led by Dave Mackay. They lost again, 3-2. For the third time that season the same scoreline had gone against Tottenham. It was only September.

Such results are often typical of teams which find themselves in trouble at the end of the season. Spurs were finding ways to lose even after having played quite well. In each match, they had scored the first goal yet still managed to lose.

After the defeat to Derby, Neill insisted that the team would finish far from the bottom, while pointing out that he still had only 13 players available because of the ongoing injury problems.

Ralph Coates was fit again after playing his way back with the reserves. Cyril Knowles also returned and went straight back into the starting line-up for the next match, a trip to Elland Road to face Leeds.

Willie Young made his debut and Spurs held the hosts to a creditable 1-1 draw.

Young was the standout again against Arsenal in his home debut. Pratt, Duncan, and McNab all went close for Spurs, but Arsenal made almost as many chances, with both goalkeepers kept busy. The match finished goalless and Tottenham had their fourth draw of the season, to go along with four defeats in nine matches.

Alfie Conn had been 'very disappointed' to be left out of the squad, having proven his fitness to return from a tendon injury by playing twice in the reserves.

Despite Spurs giving at least as good as they got, Neill was scathing afterwards, saying, 'We were disgraceful.'

The slight but noticeable upturn continued with a draw at St James' Park against a Newcastle United side which had made a comparably middling start to the season.

Conn got his chance and scored in a League Cup win over Crewe Alexandra. Bill Nicholson's final signing had made his debut for the Scottish national team the previous May, and seemed to perhaps be finally matching the high esteem in which the fans held him with his performances.

The returning Conn and joined Chivers, Coates and Don McAllister in a reshuffled Spurs side. Before the match, Conn spoke of his optimism that he could yet retain his place in the Scotland squad, saying, 'I just hope it's not too late.'

Unfortunately his goal against Crewe was the last Conn would score for Spurs. The injury would return in November to wreck his season and he would only play a minor role in the following campaign.

A trip to Villa Park followed, but the match was just a sideshow to the main event which was a remarkable refereeing performance from Kevin McNally. Terry Naylor was sent off, while five of his team-mates were booked in a remarkable refereeing performance. In the context of 1970s football this was an extraordinary amount of referee intervention.

Even the imperturbable Neill could hardly believe what he had seen, 'Naylor got sent off for doing nothing. I had a perfect view of the whole incident, and Naylor was blameless.'

Villa boss Ron Saunders was equally bemused, saying, 'People will read about all those bookings and assume there was a war on out there. In fact there was not really one bad tackle.'

Tottenham were expected to file an official complaint with the Football League over the incident, with Neill adding, 'This was a very serious day for the club and all of us who care about the image of Tottenham are extremely worried.'

The match itself finished a 1-1 draw, with John Pratt and Andy Gray scoring the goals.

Spurs passed two months without a win when they drew against Manchester City at White Hart Lane the next weekend. Jones scored twice – one from a Conn back-heel – as Tottenham flattened the visitors in the first half, but they collapsed after the break and the match finished 2-2.

Neill, who hadn't looked to have felt the pressure of a relegation battle the previous season, was fuming again and told the press to 're-use my "we were disgraceful" quotes from the Arsenal match'.

In mid-October, Cyril Knowles got the first of two testimonials. The match, against Arsenal, finished a 2-2 draw, with Knowles scoring a trademark free kick, after Don McAllister opened the scoring. Peter, Cyril's brother, who had been a Wolves and England under-23 player before retiring to work as a Jehovah's Witness missionary, came off the bench to a standing ovation. Unfortunately for Spurs, Chris Jones – who had scored three league goals after a strong pre-season – was taken off injured.

Neill restored veterans Chivers, Coates, and Neighbour to the line-up for the following match, a trip to Filbert Street to face Leicester City. The Foxes had humiliated Spurs in the same fixture the previous season, but this time Tottenham managed to win by the odd goal in five. The 12-match winless run was over and suddenly Spurs were unbeaten in six First Division games.

Tottenham won again the following weekend, beating Wolves 2-1 – a scoreline which belied their dominant display. After just four minutes Conn set a move in motion which ended with Neighbour opening the scoring. Conn then set up Jones minutes later but the young striker couldn't turn in the chance.

The Scot was running the show at White Hart Lane, but early in the second half he went down with injury and had to be replaced, before Young sealed the win with a late goal.

In November, Neill signed young striker Gerry Armstrong from Northern Irish semi-professional side Bangor. Initially it was rumoured that Armstrong had joined Spurs for a trial, but Bangor manager Bertie Neill strenuously denied those claims. Instead, Neill said Armstrong was receiving treatment for a foot injury at White Hart Lane's medical facilities.

A month later, though, Armstrong resigned from his job with the Northern Ireland Housing Executive to join Tottenham as a full-time pro.

There was a degree of irony, in light of what was to come, in the fact that Neill beat Arsenal to Armstrong's signature.

A trip to Queens Park Rangers in November saw Chivers recalled to the starting line-up, but he suffered a hamstring injury and had to be taken off midway through the goalless draw.

When the club physio got a look at the injury, Chivers says he called it 'the worst hamstring injury he had ever seen'.

Two more draws followed, in the League Cup against West Ham and away to Stoke City in the league, and Spurs were sitting in a disappointing 14th place, although some solace came from the fact that Arsenal were struggling further down in 18th.

The solid run came to an end at Maine Road. Manchester City scored two quick goals late in the match, before Osgood responded with a 35-yard peach, but it wasn't enough and the 11-match unbeaten streak was snapped. It was the first defeat suffered since the acquisition of Willie Young.

'If we'd have played as I know we can, we'd have skinned Manchester City. They're certainly not the best team we have played,' Neill said after the match.

Dave Watson, the England defender who Spurs had tried and failed to sign in the summer, was named man of the match.

Worse was the latest drama with Alfie Conn. Conn, unhappy at being on the bench, had argued with Neill on the sideline with the match in progress. The following day Neill fined Conn over the incident, while the Scot told the press, 'I can't wait to get away from Tottenham.'

Spurs then reeled off four straight wins, with John Duncan scoring eight goals. They advanced to the League Cup semi-final – their best domestic cup run in three years –

and climbed up to 11th in the table. Arsenal were continuing to struggle, flirting with relegation in 18th.

At the end of December, Cyril Knowles underwent surgery on ligaments in his left knee. He was expected to return soon but would ultimately retire before the season ended. The Everton draw was the final appearance of the 506 he made for Spurs.

Upon his retirement, only two players in the club's history had played more games – Pat Jennings and 1901 FA Cup winner Tom Morris – and only Steve Perryman and Gary Mabbutt have subsequently passed him.

18

The youth movement

GLENN HODDLE had made his debut the previous August, but he came into the team to face Stoke City on 21 February 1976 following an injury to veteran Ralph Coates. He would be an ever-present for more than a decade to come.

The 18-year-old scored his first goal in senior football with a 25-yard volley past England keeper Peter Shilton. It was a brilliant, driven shot with his left foot, rising all the time from the moment it left his boot.

Hoddle's talent was already well known and he made headlines before the match even began. He was one of four teenagers in the starting line-up, plus there was also the 20-year-old Chris Jones who had returned from injury.

Terry Neill was surprisingly downbeat on Hoddle, despite his brilliant goal. After the match, Spurs' manager said, 'There is no point in getting excited, he has so much to learn. I think he is playing for effect at the moment. He's going to be a great player, but he still has a lot to do with his game and tends to be over-elaborate. I want to see a team show rather than an individual.'

Yet again, Neill marked himself out as philosophically distant from the culture of the club he managed. Spurs fans loved the individual genius – look no further than the adoration heaped upon Alfie Conn – but Neill wanted a solid team built on sound defensive foundations.

By this point of the season, Neill was regularly fielding eight homegrown players. It was a stark contrast to the peak Bill Nicholson sides which frequently had none.

Days after the first leg of the League Cup semi-final against Newcastle, Spurs faced Manchester United at White Hart Lane. United were top of the league and nearly 50,000 fans packed the ground. The clash on the pitch ended 1-1, with John Duncan equalising for Tottenham following a lovely piece of play by McAllister, but the battle on the terraces drew greater comment.

United's travelling fans had long held a reputation as among the most 'up for it' groups of supporters. They had made headlines many times following violent scenes in and around grounds.

On this occasion, the outbreak of violence was especially severe. United fans surged on to the Shelf and Spurs supporters from all over the ground rushed in to join the fight. Some remembered seeing United fans thrown from the upper tier – miraculously escaping major injury if true – while others saw the away supporters fleeing on to the pitch. A handful of fans climbed up one of the light towers and had to be talked down by a policeman. It was a fight immortalised in a terrace song which began 'Teams I remember and teams I recall, Manchester United the greatest of all'.

Any hopes of a trophy dissolved in four disastrous days in January. First Newcastle won the second leg of the League Cup semi-final, overcoming Spurs 3-2 on aggregate, before Stoke won 2-1 to knock Tottenham out of the FA Cup.

With trophy hopes gone, Neill began to introduce more young players. Steve Walford, Mickey Stead, Martin Robinson, Noel Brotherston all made first-team appearances, and Hoddle was crossing over from young talent to regular first-team player.

In all, six youth team players were given their debut that season. Steve Perryman explained that the move towards internal development was a legacy of Bill Nicholson, whose appointment of Pat Welton was looking shrewder with every passing year.

After the evolution of transfer regulations, clubs were far more reliant on bringing their own players through. Perryman was evidence of that. Keith Osgood, John Pratt and Chris Jones, too, were first-team regulars.

Things had reached a tipping point at Tottenham. For the first time, internally developed players accounted for more – nearly 300 – appearances than those bought from other clubs.

Perryman told journalists that Nicholson 'could see the way soccer was going and realised that we would have to start finding more of our own talent. Scouting and everything was geared to producing and we are now reaping the benefit. Terry Neill … seems just as keen to carry it on and things are on the up and up.'

Reserve team manager Welton agreed, saying, 'It is encouraging for those lower down the scale – they know they may be given their chance at any moment.'

Hoddle was already seen as the greatest talent in Tottenham's youth movement, with discussion of an eventual England debut already appearing in print.

Welton, trying to calm excitement around the young midfielder, said 'It is a lot for the lad to carry. He has a long way to go but, all things being equal, he has got a chance of playing for England.'

In March, Pat Jennings was named the PFA Player of the Year. Jennings became the first non-English winner of the award, and the first goalkeeper. Having won the Football Writers' Association Footballer of the Year award in 1973, Jennings was the first player to have won both trophies.

Prince Edward, the Duke of Kent, handed the trophy to Jennings at a ceremony at the Hilton Hotel. 'This is one of the finest moments of my life. I feel very honoured,' Jennings told the press.

Not only had a goalkeeper won the individual award – a real rarity throughout football history – but Jennings was also playing for a mid-table team.

League and UEFA Cup champions Liverpool, surprise First Division contenders QPR, and Cup Winners' Cup finalists West Ham had all enjoyed far better years than Tottenham, but it was Jennings's brilliance that shone through.

A few days later, Tottenham faced Brighton in Joe Kinnear's testimonial. Jimmy Greaves, Dave Mackay and Terry Venables were invited to join the Seagulls' side for the evening, but they couldn't stop Spurs recording a rampant 6-1 win.

At the end of the month Sheffield United were thrashed 5-0 at White Hart Lane, and consequently the Blades were relegated. It was the equal biggest win of any team in the league that season. Perryman scored a rare brace, Duncan scored as usual, and even Willie Young got on the scoresheet. There was also a goal for Martin Chivers – number 174 for Tottenham. It would prove to be his last.

Spurs followed that victory with another, all the sweeter as it came against Arsenal, as the old enemy were beaten 2-0 at Highbury.

The previous season Arsenal had left Tottenham on the verge of relegation by winning this same fixture, late in the season. While Spurs would have enjoyed pushing Arsenal down into similar trouble, they had already managed to all but pull themselves clear of relegation.

The final four matches of the season brought something of a mixed return. There was a goalless draw against Leeds, a 3-1 defeat at St Andrew's against Birmingham City, a 4-1 hammering of Coventry City at White Hart Lane, and a 3-0 defeat on the final day at home against Newcastle, which was the last of 367 Tottenham appearances for Martin Chivers, albeit his involvement barely lasted for an hour.

In the 61st minute, Neill hauled Chivers off and replaced him with young Jones. Chivers was unfiltered after the match, saying, 'I was surprised and angry to be substituted and thought it was a funny decision. Everyone in the ground appeared to think so, too.'

The former England striker was not done. Referring to Neill, Chivers said, 'He always picks on me. I told him I thought it was a cowardly decision. John Duncan should have gone off, not me.'

In response, Neill admitted, 'I do pick on him and admit I'm prejudiced. And the reason is because the man has so much ability. I try to understand how he feels. Once he was the King of Europe. Now he can't score. It must be hard for him.'

Newcastle got their first goal less than a minute after the substitution was made. Young was singled out for criticism on the television coverage, with the commentator remarking that he 'has a lot to learn about First Division football. He was given the run around by [Malcolm] Macdonald, beaten hopelessly for pace'.

After a solid season which had started slowly and steadily improved, Spurs seemed to have put the worst behind them. The football wasn't spectacular and the fans had still not particularly warmed to the manager, but there was a good mix of youth and experience in the team.

After the victory over Arsenal in April, Spurs had been as high as sixth, but they ended the campaign ninth.

They had scored 63 goals, just short of league champions Liverpool's tally of 66. Only four teams had conceded more goals though, and two of those had been relegated.

Arsenal had avoided relegation. They finished 17th, and long-time manager Bertie Mee resigned. His departure would change the future of both north London clubs.

For now, Neill was working on a hugely ambitious deal to take Tottenham to the next level. He knew his team were lacking swagger and in need of a spark. He had an idea to change everything.

19

Johan Cruyff

JOHAN CRUYFF had emerged in Dutch football as a teenager at Ajax. Making his debut in 1964 at the age of 17, the Dutchman swiftly established himself.

First he became a first-team regular, then a star. He scored 25 goals in 23 games for Ajax in his first full season as a professional.

With Cruyff at the vanguard in 1966, Ajax won their first league title in six years. He would inspire them to five more in the next seven years.

When the Dutch national team was rebuilding following a fifth consecutive failure to qualify for the World Cup in England that year, Cruyff was brought into the team.

In 1971, as his star continued to rise, Cruyff won the first of three consecutive European Cups. His brilliance attracted the attention of Barcelona, where he moved for a world-record fee of $2m in 1973. There the Dutch genius led the *Blaugrana* to a thrilling league title, their first since 1960.

He won his third Ballon d'Or in four years in 1974 and shone in the brilliant Netherlands team nicknamed 'Clockwork Oranje' at the World Cup in West Germany.

The team had been built around him and the Netherlands became the greatest side to not win the World Cup, playing mesmeric, unstoppable football throughout the tournament before being upset in the final by West Germany. Cruyff then endured a frustrating second season with Barcelona in 1974/75 as Barça slumped to third in La Liga. Part of the attraction of Barcelona for Cruyff had been the presence of former Ajax coaches Vic Buckingham and Rinus Michels. Buckingham had given Cruyff his debut and made him captain of Ajax at the age of 18, forever earning the iconic Dutchman's affection.

Barcelona made a decent showing in the European Cup, losing an infamous semi-final to Leeds, and finished the season without a trophy, then Michels left to take the Netherlands national team job.

Cruyff rejected a massive contract offer from Barcelona in July 1975, with his agent telling the press that 1975/76 would be his final season in Spain.

Terry Neill, once again benefiting from his network of contacts, learned that Cruyff wanted to play in England, and particularly for Spurs. Cruyff had the connection to Tottenham of Buckingham, a former Spurs player.

Contact was opened with Cruyff's agent Denis Roach and Neill began working out the practicalities of a move. Owing to Cruyff's contract situation, the required fee would have been just under £300,000. That was still a large sum but far less than what he had cost when leaving Ajax.

Neill said the Dutch playmaker had expressed 'a keen interest' in joining. The only major hurdle was seemingly Cruyff's wage demands. The Dutch icon would want a salary in line with his status as one of the world's finest players, and Tottenham simply did not have that kind of money to offer.

Neill hit upon a unique solution, contacting numerous British companies to organise sponsorship deals which would top up Cruyff's salary. In talks, Cruyff apparently told Neill that he 'could never find a better platform to play in England than Spurs'.

Knowing that secrecy was of the utmost importance to the deal, Neill had opted to keep Tottenham's board in the dark.

In February, Cruyff was openly insulting Barcelona manager Hennes Weisweiler in the press. That same month, the *Daily Mirror* reported that Spurs had approached the Dutch star. When pressed by reporters, Neill confirmed that he was trying to pull off the stunning transfer and was prepared to fight the FA's ban on foreign players, citing the Treaty of Rome's freedom of movement clause.

A furious board confronted Neill, who said they accused him of 'deception' and called his attempts to sign a player without their knowledge 'outrageous'.

The board's implacable anger meant that any deal was dead in the water, and Tottenham missed out on signing one of the great icons of 20th-century football.

Instead of leaving, Cruyff extended his contract with Barcelona in April. That season he scored 25 goals for Barcelona, and only retired eight years – and six trophies – later.

It is no overstatement to say that the history of European football would have been quite different if Spurs had signed a 29-year-old Cruyff in 1976.

Even when he returned to the Netherlands in the 1980s, Cruyff remained a force. He led Ajax to an Eredivisie title, then a league and cup double. In 1983/84, his final season as a professional, he crossed the fiery divide between Ajax and rivals Feyenoord, following a customary disagreement with the Amsterdam club's board. In Rotterdam, Cruyff was still a supreme player. He led Feyenoord to a double of their own, and was en route to a treble until being eliminated from the UEFA Cup by Tottenham.

It was not the last highly ambitious deal which Neill would attempt to pull off. He tried to sign Diego Maradona and even Glenn Hoddle after the manager had left Tottenham for Arsenal in 1976. Hoddle admitted later that he could have crossed north London, but said, 'I don't think my brother would have ever spoken to me again if I had.'

Nor was it the last time that Tottenham would try to beat more fancied clubs to the signing of a prestigious foreign star.

20

Neill crosses north London

BERTIE MEE had been a Royal Army physiotherapist during the Second World War, and joined Arsenal in the same role in 1960. When Billy Wright – the former England captain and star of the iconic Wolverhampton Wanderers team of the 1950s – was sacked, the Gunners turned to their physio and handed him the top job. Mee, never renowned for his tactical prowess, leaned heavily on coaches already at the club, but performed admirably.

Legendary writer Brian Glanville – who continued his practice of dictating football copy down the telephone from his bath until well into the 2010s – wrote that Mee won the love of his squad when he threw himself into a brawl between Arsenal and Lazio players after a European match in 1970.

He took those players to two League Cup finals in the late 1960s, but lost to Leeds United and Swindon Town respectively.

He signed George Graham, he brought through Charlie George, and he inculcated a careful, risk-averse style of football. In 1970/71, Mee's approach paid off handsomely as Arsenal followed Tottenham in winning the Double.

Five years later, after several years in the wilderness, Mee had resigned and the Gunners were looking for a new manager. Real Madrid coach Miljan Miljanić was their initial target, and on 20 April 1976 he was pictured at Heathrow after flying in for talks.

Miljanić had spent time with Bill Nicholson in the late 1960s, attempting to refine his own coaching style and to learn what he could about the 1961 Tottenham team.

The Yugoslavian had led Red Star Belgrade to the semi-finals of the European Cup and the quarter-finals of the Cup Winners' Cup before moving to Madrid. He won back-to-back La Liga titles in Spain, as well as the Copa del Generalisimo in 1975 and had been in 1976 the inaugural winner of the Don Balón Award for the best coach in Spain.

Miljanić was famous for the intensity of his preparation, both in physical and tactical terms. Vicente del Bosque, Spain's World Cup-winning coach in 2010, considered Miljanić a pioneer.

What Arsène Wenger would be for English football decades later – a modern shock to a moribund system – Miljanić might have been in the 1970s, but the deal fell through.

Terry Venables had retired as a player and was looking for a first managerial role, but he too had rejected an offer from Arsenal.

Running out of ideas, and time, Arsenal set their focus on Terry Neill. Despite the solid season and general improvement, Neill's ongoing issues with the Spurs board and the running of the club continued to eat away at him. The failure of the move for Johan Cruyff also could not have helped Neill to feel settled or valued by his directors.

Ralph Coates, Jimmy Neighbour, John Pratt, Keith Osgood and goalkeeper Barry Daines had all rejected the new contracts offered by the club, adding to building pressure.

Neill then endured misery on a summer trip to Australia, clashing with the board over their treatment of the players and what he perceived to be their miserly approach.

On the pitch, Spurs had been in fine form, winning nine games out of nine including a 3-2 victory over the Australian national team. Martin Chivers had been injured in a match in Fiji, trapping his studs in a concrete cricket pitch – covered in wood shavings for safety – in the middle of the field and missed most of the tour.

Behind closed doors, Neill was fed up with the board. The high-handed treatment of backroom staff particularly rankled Neill, and the directors' failure to invite the players to a champagne luncheon during the tour was a final straw.

Throughout the tour, Neill had had disputes with many of his players, too. Chivers, injured early on, was thankful for Neill's decision to simply ignore him.

Glenn Hoddle, for his part, was completely fed up with his treatment by Neill. He felt that the manager blamed him or fellow youngster Steve Walford for everything that went wrong on that tour. Hoddle felt that this was a deliberate attempt to highlight his authority to the other players. Regardless of the reasoning behind it, Hoddle had made up his mind that he would leave Tottenham to get away from Neill.

Spurs had reached a real potential turning point. The board were probably not aware of the stakes involved, but it was clear that hard choices loomed for those involved.

With tension boiling over, Neill told chairman Sidney Wale that he was resigning. In this critical situation, Wale refused to delay his holiday and departed for the south coast.

Charles Fox, the club's vice-chairman, was left to deal with the Neill problem himself and rejected the resignation outright.

Two weeks after quitting, Neill remained in a fully uncertain position, telling reporters, 'I have no idea what I am going to do, but I am determined to leave Tottenham.'

While confusion dominated the situation at Spurs, Arsenal chairman Denis Hill-Wood moved to offer Neill the chance to replace Mee at Highbury. He told newspapers that Neill's resignation from Tottenham was 'very interesting'.

After his third attempt to quit, Neill took his board dispute public, telling the *Daily Mirror*, 'My resignation is an accumulation of frustrations. The board are fully aware of my reasons.'

Neill still had 14 months left on the three-year contract that he had signed when taking over from Bill Nicholson but he was quite insistent that he would not continue.

He had still not left White Hart Lane, but he was already the bookmakers' favourite to take over at Highbury.

At the end of June, Wale returned from his holiday and the Tottenham board finally accepted the inevitable. Neill was gone. Spurs made an official statement, saying mysteriously that the 'major differences between Mr Neill and the Board related to certain proposals made by Mr Neill concerning payments which he wished to make to some of its employees'.

Neill apparently interpreted Tottenham's statement as implying that he had suggested under-the-table payments. Neill gave a response of his own, rejecting this idea, 'At no time did I advocate illegal or improper payments. I requested the board to consider legitimate methods to assist players' financial position.' He also accused Spurs' board of 'complete lack of response to my requests and grievances'.

When the news broke, Hoddle – on the verge of forcing his way out – was suddenly happy to stay. Steve Perryman – Neill's captain – was stunned, saying, 'It has come right out of the blue. The only explanation I can think of is that he wanted to buy somebody and the board refused to let him have the money. Things just seemed to be going well.'

Things had been going particularly well for Perryman. The two seasons under Neill had seen him first recover his best form and then grow as a player. He scored 13 goals under Neill, and would average fewer than two per year for the rest of his career. Wale claimed Neill 'knew nothing about the Arsenal job' when he first tried to quit. Neill himself always maintained that he had not yet pursued the role before resigning.

Atlético Madrid and Athletic Bilbao were mentioned in the papers as potential options for Neill's next club. Neill himself admitted that he could not afford to stay out of the game for long, saying, 'I'm in a difficult position. I have a family to provide for.'

On 9 July Neill was installed at Highbury. He became Arsenal's youngest ever manager, and would lead the Gunners to four finals, including three straight FA Cup finals from 1978 to 1980, winning the 1979 showpiece. Former Gunners player Neill described Arsenal as 'my spiritual home, and nothing else could ever come close to them'.

Neill was gone and the Tottenham board once again found themselves short on applicants for a new manager. For whatever reason, they refused to approach other potential candidates, and simply awaited applications. When no suitable candidates presented themselves, the board turned to first-team coach Keith Burkinshaw.

Before he left though, Neill had finally succeeded in getting rid of Martin Chivers. The former England striker was sent to Servette in Switzerland. Upon hearing the name and location of his next club, Chivers asked Neill, 'Is that far enough away for you?'

If Nicholson and Chivers had had a complex relationship, there was little complexity to that of Chivers and Bill's successor; they simply couldn't stand each other.

While Nicholson and Chivers resolved their difference after the striker retired, and became very close in their later years, Chivers and Neill never passed anything more than the minimum courtesies between them again.

Chivers, for his part, said he had 'never known such a disorganised bunch of players' as Tottenham under Neill.

Speaking years later, Chivers said of himself, Mike England, Martin Peters and the other veteran players, 'We were forced out. I don't know how the club ever took him on.'

Chivers' disdain even extended to the players brought in by Neill. He considered Willie Young 'a donkey' and John Duncan 'an awful player who never passed to anybody'.

Neill had been trying to move Chivers on for several years and he had told him he would be sold in 1975. It was Neill's final act of consequence for Tottenham, sealing the deal with Servette even after returning from Australia.

Chivers did make an appearance in the last match of the tour, where he scored a hat-trick against Western Australia. It was his final game in a Tottenham shirt.

When Chivers heard that Neill had resigned, he went to Wale's house to beg him to cancel the deal. He wanted to stay at Spurs, but Wale refused to break the agreement and Chivers was gone. Chivers left as Tottenham's third-highest goalscorer. Only Jimmy Greaves and Bobby Smith had scored more, and in the nearly 50 years since he left, only Harry Kane has since passed him. Neill's legacy at Tottenham is complex. The list of managers to successfully replace a club legend is short. Real Madrid won the first five European Cups, running through five different managers in the process. Ajax replaced Rinus Michels with Ștefan Kovács, extending a run of two European Cup wins to three.

The Liverpool 'boot room' system that produced a run of Bill Shankly, Bob Paisley, Joe Fagan and Kenny Dalglish – each of whom won at least one league title – is the ultimate example, but there are few others.

Typically, taking on a job like Neill did leads to failure. Alex Ferguson, Arsène Wenger, José Mourinho, Matt Busby – four of the five most successful managers in English football during the postwar period – each saw their successors – David Moyes, Unai Emery, Avram Grant, and Wilf McGuinness respectively – flounder.[21] None of those icons' replacements

---

21 Bob Paisley is the missing name from that list, being replaced by the comparably successful Joe Fagan.

brought with them the baggage of being a legend of a rival club.

It is difficult to say whether Neill really did fail. The Spurs squad he inherited was ageing and in need of an overhaul. Trophy wins in the early 1970s had helped disguise the fact that Bill Nicholson's final team was nothing like as strong as the earlier editions.

Neill helped keep Tottenham up in his first season in charge, and managed a solid second season, but – apart from one League Cup run – he never threatened to win a trophy. He also fell out with many of his star players and walked out on a squad he had only partially finished rebuilding weeks before a new season in which they would face disaster.

It is impossible to know whether Tottenham would have fared better in 1976/77 if Neill had stayed in his post, but they could hardly have done worse.

21

Spurs give it to 'Mr Who'

THE LAST time that Tottenham had changed manager, Danny Blanchflower had been the popular favourite but didn't get the job. This time Blanchflower did take a managerial position – just not at Spurs.

On 16 June 1976, Blanchflower began his tenure in charge of the Northern Ireland national team. His message was, as ever, that attacking football was key. He said, 'These players have been too defensive-minded. They are ingrained in defensive habits and I've got to attempt to introduce an attacking flair.'

Once again Tottenham were looking for a new manager, and once again they were short on applicants.

Gordon Jago, one of the candidates to replace Bill Nicholson in 1974, had subsequently moved to Millwall and guided them to promotion. He was again mentioned as an option in the press. So too, were Alan Mullery, ex-Palace boss Malcolm Allison, and former Burnley coach Jimmy Adamson. Allison had won four major trophies as Manchester City manager, and would go on to success with Sporting in Portugal.

Others suggested as likely candidates included Leeds coach Don Howe, Charlton Athletic's Andy Nelson and Sir Alf Ramsey.

One name not being mentioned was Keith Burkinshaw. The extent to which Burkinshaw was an unknown quantity can be seen in the fact that his only mention in the coverage of Terry Neill's departure was in suggestions that 'Steve Burkinshaw' would probably also make the switch to Highbury.

By 13 July the newspapers were getting Burkinshaw's name right, but still only in reports suggesting he was very likely to leave Tottenham and be part of Neill's coaching setup at Arsenal. It came as a shock then, when Tottenham announced him as their new manager 24 hours later.

The 41-year-old had been put through the emotional wringer in the preceding weeks. When news of Neill's resignation reached him, Burkinshaw admitted that he expected to be out of a job, 'I was on holiday in Spain when I heard. I just thought, here we go again. I thought I would have to start looking round.'

The Yorkshireman stood – shirtless – alongside chairman Sidney Wale as he was announced to the players as their new manager.

Perryman, made captain by Neill, had led a players' deputation to the board, insisting that Burkinshaw be given the job. On the day of Burkinshaw's appointment, the number one song on the billboard chart was 'Afternoon Delight' by the Starland Vocal Band. Delighted, and surprised, Tottenham's 15th full time manager spoke to the press, 'Amazing how it turns out. One minute you are out of a job, the next you're in charge of one of the best-known clubs in the world. I didn't think I would get this job but I thought I would apply because I felt I was as good as anyone. It is a big job, a really big one. But I don't want to dwell on that too much. If I did, the thought of it might scare me to death.'

From his first public statement, Burkinshaw was saying the right things. Getting the fans on his side would be imperative to any hopes of success and a slight exaggeration of Tottenham's status – in the mid-1970s they were hardly in the first rank of elite clubs – was a good way to begin.

The humble new boss told reporters, 'The ironic thing is that if someone else had been appointed, I might easily have found myself out of work. Now I'm the manager at one of the game's great clubs. That's the way this game goes.'

Burkinshaw also gave some insight into what would drive him as a manager. His apprenticeship had been long, but that gradual ascent had finally brought him to the job he wanted, 'What satisfies me most is that at last I have got a boss's job. I have always found it a bit frustrating helping to influence decisions but never being able to make the final one. Now I will have the chance to determine my own destination and that is an important thing.'

If Burkinshaw felt he was ready for the job, the newspapers did not share his optimism. The front page of the *Daily Mirror*'s sport section the next morning read 'Spurs give it to "Mr Who"'. Burkinshaw himself admitted that fans would be saying, 'Keith who?'

In truth, Burkinshaw's success in coaching roles from Workington to Tottenham had given him a strong reputation inside the game. Just as they had in his time at at Newcastle United, the Spurs players had grown very fond of him. The well-informed *Mirror* reporter Harry Miller suggested that Burkinshaw would have been the players' choice.

Neill's departure had come just 38 days before the start of the new season. It might have been expected to unsettle the team, but Neill was so unpopular with many of the players that his replacement by the comparatively beloved Burkinshaw probably improved the atmosphere at the club.

One of Burkinshaw's first acts upon being appointed was revealing. After less than a week in the job he called Bill Nicholson and asked him to return to Tottenham Hotspur.

While Burkinshaw exuded humility in his public statements, he clearly did not lack for confidence. Willingly bringing in Nicholson – a manager whose achievements could not realistically be improved upon – showed a fearlessness and self-belief that Burkinshaw would need in the lean early months of his tenure.

It was also another shrewd move in political terms. The return of Nicholson would surely buy him a little more goodwill among the supporters.

Nicholson had been working for Ron Greenwood's West Ham but happily agreed to go back as a football consultant. He was plainly delighted to do so, saying, 'I've never lost interest in Spurs and it's great to be back. Keith is young and I hope he looks to me for advice and help. I'll probably be involved in scouting and administrative work.' In fact, Nicholson would be hugely influential in this new role.

Like many successful managers, Burkinshaw had been an honest, workmanlike player – far from a star. Glenn Hoddle said of him, 'He wanted to create a team that could be all of the things he wasn't.'

Burkinshaw was in many ways a traditionalist. Like Nicholson, he was committed to attacking, entertaining football above all. However, in at least one way he was also an iconoclast. He refused to be called 'boss' or 'gaffer' by his players. Instead, he said, 'My name is Keith, call me that.'

In his autobiography, Nicholson stressed that any success under Burkinshaw should be credited to Burkinshaw – not to him – but there is no doubt that the return of the iconic manager provided a spark for the club.

After restoring Nicholson, Burkinshaw's next move was to bring Pat Welton into his coaching team. Tottenham's first team, already full of homegrown talent, would continue to benefit from Welton's influence in the coming years.

The good feeling at the club did not last though and whatever credit there was to be shared around would be thin on the ground for some time.

In August, John Duncan underwent a back operation which would keep him out for the first two months of the season, and subsequently flare up multiple times throughout the difficult campaign.

Duncan had been top scorer the past two seasons, scoring 37 goals, but would manage just four in nine appearances in 1976/77.

With Martin Chivers gone and Duncan out, Tottenham were missing a true number nine. But what they did have was a significant transfer budget. The sale of Chivers, and advance season ticket sales, had generated around £300,000.

The obvious and widely reported target was Newcastle striker Malcolm 'Supermac' Macdonald. Burkinshaw had known Macdonald from his years coaching the Magpies, and Neill had already opened preliminary discussions to bring the prolific goalscorer to London before walking out on Tottenham.

Unfortunately for Spurs, Neill retained his interest in Macdonald and made a decisive move to take him to Highbury while Spurs were in West Germany on a pre-season tour.

Spurs tried to sign David Johnson, offering £200,000 for the Ipswich and England striker, but he rejected them in favour of a move to Liverpool where he would win four league titles and three European Cups.

Instead, Tottenham bought Ian Moores from Stoke City for £80,000.

Gerry Armstrong made his debut in a season-opening 3-1 defeat at Ipswich with Barry Daines selected in goal due to Pat Jennings's injury-enforced absence. Daines kept his place for the next match with Jennings still sidelined and Spurs lost again, 2-0 at home to Newcastle.

They got their first point of the season in a goalless draw with Middlesbrough, before beating Boro three days later in the League Cup. Moores scored on his debut.

Despite the results, Burkinshaw was committed to an attacking style of play and would not be convinced to alter his approach.

Moores scored again in a 3-2 win over Manchester United – Burkinshaw's first victory in the First Division. United had hammered Spurs in the first half but somehow failed to score. Steve Perryman said afterwards that his team had been sparked into action by their embarrassment. They scored their three goals from three shots. Stunned United manager Tommy Docherty said after the match, 'I can't believe it.'

A week later, Chris Jones got the only goal against Leeds as Spurs won back-to-back league games before Jennings returned, but the results deteriorated again. Liverpool won 2-0 at Anfield before Wrexham knocked Spurs out of the League Cup.

Still unable to find a striker, Burkinshaw signed Peter Taylor for £200,000 from Crystal Palace. The winger had broken into the England team as a Third Division player in 1973, but with Palace drowning in debt, new manager Terry Venables made him available for transfer. Arsenal, Leeds and Everton had all considered moves for Taylor, but Burkinshaw moved fastest.

Burkinshaw then sold Jimmy Neighbour to Norwich for £75,000. Neighbour, who had been in the first team for six years and notably started the 1971 League Cup Final win over Villa, actually made his final appearance for Spurs in a draw against the team he was about to join.

Taylor made a goalscoring debut in a 4-2 defeat to West Bromwich Albion before Duncan then delivered a rare piece of good news, declaring himself fit ahead of schedule. But it turned out to be premature.

Duncan made his first appearance of the season on 9 October in Peter Simpson's testimonial match. He scored the opener as Spurs won 2-1 but wasn't yet fit enough to play in a competitive game. In the same match, defender Willie Young also returned from an injury suffered a month earlier. Things appeared to be looking up, at last, but then came a particularly unpleasant trip to Derbyshire.

22

Historic humiliation

DERBY COUNTY, two years removed from winning the First Division under Dave Mackay, welcomed Spurs to the Baseball Ground on 16 October 1976 and handed them an 8-2 humiliation. Charlie George, the ex-Arsenal star who had come so close to joining Spurs, scored twice. Bruce Rioch scored four goals.

Derby were struggling – in fact Mackay would be sacked within a month – but they destroyed Tottenham all the same.

Keith Burkinshaw was still tinkering with his defence, not satisfied with the starting partnership of Keith Osgood and Willie Young. Against Derby he experimented with John Pratt as a sweeper in behind. This new tactic did not pay dividends.

It was 3-2 to Derby at half-time, and the talk in the dressing room was optimism at digging out a result, but the Rams fired in five more goals in 13 second-half minutes as Spurs fell to pieces.

It was Tottenham's record defeat. Burkinshaw kept the team in the dressing room for an hour and 20 minutes after the match. He began by pointing out all the mistakes the players had made, but then shifted, saying to the team, 'I wonder if you care. Will you wake up tomorrow morning and think about being beaten 8-2? Do you care about playing for Tottenham; what sort of club Tottenham are; what position they hold in football?'

Defeats of that magnitude are often the end of a manager's time at a club. The fact that Burkinshaw not only survived, but would eventually stay in the job for eight years, suggests that perhaps his speech that day did have an effect on his players.

On leaving the dressing room, Burkinshaw, head down, just said 'no comment' and continued down the hall, straight past the waiting reporters. Later he said 'I have a deep sense of shame and regret.'

Pat Jennings, the last Tottenham player to emerge, could only mumble the word 'nightmare'. Captain Steve Perryman was more forthcoming, explaining a few days after the match, 'A lot of people were hurt on Saturday – our pride was hurt. We all felt ashamed. Now we have an opportunity to put things right. There will be a big improvement in our performance. We owe it to the manager.'

Later, Perryman also said that Jennings had been the best player on the pitch, saying he 'performed miracles. Without him it could have been 20–2'.

Burkinshaw responded to the destruction at Derby by dropping Alfie Conn and Terry Naylor, handing apprentice defender Andy Keeley his debut in the next match, at home to Birmingham City – one of just six appearances he would make for Spurs – and bringing McAllister back into the team. Spurs did improve, recording a rare clean sheet as they beat Birmingham 1-0. As they struggled towards victory, the performance of 18-year-old Glenn Hoddle was notable. While his team-mates looked unconfident, fearful and clumsy, Hoddle impressed with his skill and bravery in possession.

Duncan returned again in a 3-3 draw with Everton, becoming the 20th different player to start a match in the league for Spurs that season. At a time when squads were still quite modest – certainly by modern standards – this was a remarkable tally to reach before November.

In November, centre-back Osgood became Tottenham's leading scorer for the campaign with a brace in a win over Stoke.

After Everton, Spurs lost three straight games. A 2-0 home win over Stoke City provided some respite, lifting Tottenham off the bottom of the table. A draw against Manchester City then followed courtesy of a Taylor brace.

A derby draw against Arsenal and a 2-1 win over West Ham – matches in which Duncan scored twice – got Spurs up to 18th, two points away from the relegation places as 1977 came around. At that point, Tottenham had only lost once in six weeks and seemed to be finding their way out of danger.

In January, chairman Sidney Wale spoke to Burkinshaw to assure him that his job was not in jeopardy. While this sort of action has become known as the 'dreaded vote of confidence' and can usually be expected to precede a manager's removal, in this case Wale kept his word.

Shortly after Wale's announcement, however, Spurs' form disappeared. They lost five of their next six league matches – and were knocked out of the FA Cup by Cardiff City – and slid all the way down to the bottom of the table.

Things got worse when Jennings succumbed to a groin injury which would keep him out for most of the next two months.

23

Dead men walking

IN MARCH, back-to-back wins gave Spurs renewed hope. In the first, 3-1 against Norwich City, Keith Burkinshaw switched Steve Perryman into defence for the first time. While he struggled early on – Norwich took the lead and could have scored three – the move was a revelation. Perryman's ability on the ball gave the team an outlet from the back and his positional sense, once adjusted, helped steady an unreliable back line.

The next game was against Kevin Keegan and Liverpool; Spurs pulled off a huge upset, winning 1-0. The Reds were top of the league and on their way to another title, but Ralph Coates scored the only goal as Tottenham pulled themselves out of the relegation zone, moving up to 18th.

Alfie Conn left the club in March, joining Celtic for £65,000. He took a pay cut from £240 per week to £70. The former Rangers midfielder became the first player in 50 years to play for both Old Firm clubs. He had made 13 appearances that season, but had been largely playing second-string football. Legendary Celtic manager Jock Stein made the journey down to London to watch Conn play for the reserves against Hereford.

Conn, who had been popular with the fans but an irregular starter since joining in 1974, was an instant success back in Scotland. He won the First Division and League Cup in his first full season.

However, his successful return came at a cost, with Rangers fans never forgiving him for crossing the Glasgow divide. Only four players have subsequently done likewise.

Willie Young also left his struggling team-mates to join former manager Terry Neill at Arsenal for £80,000 – less than half of the fee Spurs had paid to sign him. Young conceded a penalty in a debut defeat against Ipswich Town but would go on to greater success at Highbury than he had had at White Hart Lane.

Three days after beating the champions-to-be, Spurs lost at home to West Bromwich Albion. Next they travelled to St Andrew's and beat Birmingham City, before earning a goalless draw against Derby.

Spurs were again 18th, temporarily out of trouble, but they were slapped 4-0 by Everton in the next match and just two points from the drop zone.

On 9 April Spurs faced Queens Park Rangers in a must-win match. QPR were also relegation candidates and were missing Stan Bowles, Gerry Francis and Frank McLintock through injury. Coates and Glenn Hoddle ran Spurs' midfield and a largely one-sided match was decided in 90 second-half seconds when Chris Jones scored twice.

The victory, padded out to 3-0 when Peter Taylor scored late, took Spurs up to 17th. It was a congested table and all of the bottom nine teams – separated by just eight points – were in potential danger.

Two days after that result, Spurs crossed north London to face Arsenal. For the third successive season the late-season clash between the rivals held relegation implications for one of the clubs involved. Terry Neill's Gunners were comfortably mid-table and had the opportunity to deal a sizeable blow to the survival hopes of Spurs.

The night before the derby, Arsenal striker Malcolm Macdonald was forced to undergo an emergency dental procedure on an infected abscess.

Keith Burkinshaw had tried to sign Macdonald from Newcastle the previous summer. He knew how dangerous the prolific, speedy striker could be, having coached him on Tyneside. Macdonald had once scored five goals in a single match for England.

Neill had actually begun Tottenham's work to sign MacDonald before crossing the divide, but beat Burkinshaw to the deal after heading to Highbury with Macdonald moving to Arsenal instead.

Macdonald scored three goals in his first four games, before hitting a hat-trick against his former club, showing exactly the scoring quality that Spurs so badly lacked in the absence of John Duncan.

Despite a sleepless night, and swollen face, Macdonald started against Tottenham. His presence would prove decisive.

The derby was, as so many in this period, an ugly affair. Willie Young was forced off briefly in the first half following a head clash with Chris Jones. After receiving four stitches, the bloodied Young returned to the pitch.

With the match looking likely to peter out into a draw, a routine Osgood clearance rebounded off Perryman and fell into the path of Macdonald. Barry Daines got a hand to Macdonald's shot and pushed it wide for a corner, receiving the biggest cheer of the day.

Minutes later though, Osgood's under-hit back-pass gave Macdonald the perfect chance. He stole in and slipped the ball under Daines for the winner, and his 20th goal of the season. Macdonald had also scored a brace in the reverse fixture, a 2-2 draw in December.

To make matters worse, Coates – who had played so well against QPR – split his shin open and was unable to recover in time for the next match.

Defeat at Highbury dropped Spurs down to 21st, but the following day's trip to bottom club Bristol City was a chance to recover some ground. Victory would renew hopes of another great escape like the one conjured by Neill two years before, while defeat would all but consign Spurs to relegation.

It was a tight affair at Ashton Gate. Both sides came close, Taylor notably curling one effort just wide in the first half. The hosts had the ball in the net just before the hour mark but the goal was ruled out for handball.

A few minutes later, Terry Naylor conceded a 'needless' penalty, and Bristol City striker Peter Cormack scored from the spot. Spurs were beaten and now almost certainly down.

After the match, Burkinshaw was critical of Naylor, saying, 'Terry didn't need to bring [him] down. We were under no pressure at the time.'

The Spurs boss also had words for the Football League, questioning why Spurs faced such a congested fixture list – they played seven matches in the first 20 days of April – when other clubs had nothing like such a busy calendar, 'I can't see why we have to play so many crucial games on top of one another. Players have no chance to get fit and the league shouldn't impose this on us.'

Far from getting fit, Spurs' injury problems worsened with defender Jimmy Holmes injuring ankle ligaments in the first half against Bristol.

On the same night, 19-year-old striker Garth Crooks scored a brace for Stoke City in a 2-1 win over Leeds which took them out of range of Tottenham. Only a miracle could save the Lilywhites this time.

24

We will return

WITH SIX games remaining, Tottenham's situation was critical but there was still a glimmer of hope. The visit of Sunderland, fellow relegation candidates, was another opportunity for Spurs to begin to extricate themselves from their deep pit of trouble, but they could manage only a draw. Match reports had the feel of obituaries for Tottenham, reflecting on their former glories and how low they had now fallen.

Defeat at Aston Villa followed, then Arsenal captain Pat Rice declared that the Gunners wanted to help Spurs avoid the drop, arguing that their loss would be bad for the First Division. The Gunners promptly beat Coventry City 2-0, leaving the Sky Blues on the same points as Spurs, albeit with four games in hand.

Pat Jennings finally made his return from injury for the following match, against Stoke City. Spurs got a goalless draw which moved them out of the drop zone again.

They had just three games left, while their relegation rivals Coventry, West Ham and Bristol City had seven, six and seven respectively. Despite having played so many more matches, Spurs had only a one-point buffer.

Glenn Hoddle shone in a 3-1 win over Aston Villa, played just ten days after the reverse fixture. He said that the match had the feeling of a major European night, and that afterwards the players felt the euphoria of possibility. They believed could escape the drop.

That victory had given Spurs a lifeline but, with just two matches remaining, 7 May was to be the decisive day as Spurs travelled to Manchester City knowing that only victory would do, and even then results would have to go their way.

City had beaten Newcastle United to win the 1976 League Cup – the same match that eventually saw Keith Burkinshaw sacked – and the subsequent arrival of Brian Kidd from Arsenal for £100,000 had strengthened an already solid side.

They were pushing Liverpool for the league title, and enjoying their best season since winning the championship in 1968.

Much like in 1975, Tottenham's only hope was to beat a far stronger side, only this time there was no looming European final to distract their opponent.

Spurs fell behind midway through the first half, and all hope was gone when City added three more without reply in a 12-minute burst just after the break. Kidd added a fifth and Tottenham were effectively down.

Not only had Tottenham been humiliated – again – but none of the other results had gone their way. Bristol City got a point against Manchester United, Stoke did likewise at home to Norwich City, and West Ham matched their rivals' results with a 2-2 draw against Derby, as did Queens Park Rangers at home to eventual champions Liverpool. Sunderland even pulled off a victory against Birmingham.

After the match, despite the mathematical possibility of survival, Burkinshaw admitted that it was over and seemingly felt that his time in charge might be, too. 'Tottenham are a great club and I can say without doubt that, whoever is in charge in the future, the team will soon be back,' he said after the match.

Four days later, Stoke picked up a point which meant Spurs could not catch them. Only West Ham remained in range. The Hammers had to travel to Anfield to face treble-chasing Liverpool before welcoming Manchester United to Upton Park.

For Spurs to stay up, West Ham would have to lose both matches by significant margins. Even then, QPR and Bristol City had enough games in hand to relegate both London clubs. Despite Burkinshaw's pronouncement, there remained a tiny flicker of hope.

Liverpool needed a point to secure their tenth league title – the most in English history – and they set out like a team meaning to do so against the Hammers.

With thousands of fans locked out and Anfield heaving in the warm spring weather, the ambulance men were kept busy carrying out fainting supporters.

There was a party atmosphere in the stands but tension on the pitch as the Reds dominated from the opening whistle but could not find the breakthrough.

Resolute defending held out against the rising tide of Liverpool attacks and the match finished as a goalless draw. Both sides got what they needed. Liverpool were champions, West Ham were safe and Tottenham were down. The miracle of 1974 could not be repeated.

At the same time that their fate was being decided elsewhere, Spurs were beating Leicester City at White Hart Lane.

Jimmy Holmes – signed from Coventry for £120,000 in March – scored the opening goal. A loose back-pass from Taylor almost allowed Leicester to equalise but Jennings kept his final clean sheet for Tottenham, in his 472nd league appearance.

John Pratt scored Spurs' second, collecting the rebound after his own initial shot hit the post, and Tottenham bade farewell to the First Division with a victory.

More than 26,000 people had filled White Hart Lane for what they knew before kick-off would be a goodbye to the top flight. Before the match the atmosphere was strange, almost celebratory. At full time, fans stormed on to the pitch. A large banner which read 'We Will Return' was carried around the ground.

Supporters who were there remember the day far differently from how a typical relegation is experienced, especially one for a club for whom it had come as such a shock.

Spurs' 27-year stay in the First Division was, at the time, the second-longest run in the league. Only Arsenal had been in the top flight for longer.

Antony Beevor has written that nothing is inevitable in history, except in hindsight, and that can be seen in Tottenham's relegation.

A series of small disasters had culminated in a cataclysm. Tottenham could perhaps have survived losing their iconic goalkeeper for much of the season. The failure to replace the goals of the departed Martin Chivers need not have been a mortal blow. The injury to John Duncan, too. Even the appointment, in desperation, of an untried manager on the eve of the season might have been survivable. But put all together though, Spurs had taken too many hits to stay up.

Tottenham had actually picked up six points from their final six games, and five in four since Jennings's return.

His absence, always likely to be costly, had proven decisive. Barry Daines had kept just seven clean sheets from 19 appearances, whereas Jennings had ten in 23. Jennings's impact on the team – his veteran leadership, ability to conjure points from nothing – was sorely missed.

Under today's system of three points for a win, Tottenham would have stayed up by a single point and Bristol City would have gone down in their place. They had scored as many goals – 48 – as tenth-placed Leeds, but conceded 72 – easily the worst in the division.

Burkinshaw's commitment to attacking football was admirable, and very much in keeping with the philosophy of the club, but he simply didn't have the quality in his squad. A more conservative approach might have seen Spurs limp over the line, but that was not the manager's style.

The lack of a reliable goalscorer had proven decisive. Twenty-two-year-old Chris Jones was the top scorer with just nine league goals in 31 appearances. Peter Taylor chipped in with eight, while penalty taking defender Keith Osgood added seven more. No other player managed more than four. John Duncan, who had scored 25 goals the previous season, managed just nine league appearances and two goals.

For Steve Perryman, relegation came almost as a relief. Tottenham had been a poor team for years.

Under Bill Nicholson the trophies had continued to arrive, helping to obscure the overall descent of the team. The inability of Nicholson and his successors to acquire quality players, despite often having the money to pay for them, demonstrated how widespread was the sense that Tottenham were no longer a top club.

Relegation for Manchester United two years earlier had been something of a blessing in disguise. The former European champions had quickly rebuilt their team, been promoted immediately and gone close to winning the First Division title in their first season back in the division.

Perhaps Spurs could do the same.

25

Burkinshaw's blunder

THE EMERGENCE of Barry Daines, and the injury issues which had kept Pat Jennings out for half the season, meant Keith Burkinshaw was faced with a difficult decision.

Jennings knew that Daines had done well, and accepted himself that he was approaching the age where most goalkeepers begin to decline. But Jennings was not most goalkeepers. He had twice been named in the PFA First Division Team of the Year, most recently in 1976. His contract was running down and his place in the team was in question for the first time.

Despite the uncertainty, Jennings asked for a loan of £10,000 to help him buy a house. He assumed Spurs would handle it but they refused, citing the already completed budget as justification. That refusal was his first hint that perhaps the club was seriously considering moving on from him.

Negotiations over a new contract had also not been going well. Jennings had asked for a two-year contract, while Spurs were offering only a one-year extension. Despite the contractual stalemate, Jennings was shocked to learn that Burkinshaw had decided to go with Daines, saying later, 'All of a sudden I was made available for transfer.'

Jennings didn't want to leave, but Burkinshaw had made his mind up and had no interest in courting controversy by benching a club legend. Better, thought Burkinshaw, to make a clean break.

The giant goalkeeper – in both stature and reputation – had many offers, but chose the one which he felt would best underline the mistake the club was making, 'I chose to go to Arsenal because ... I knew it would cause the biggest embarrassment to the manager who made me available.'

One enduring, though never fully confirmed, story from this period elucidates the situation. With Jennings sure he was leaving, but not yet decided on where he would go, he went to see off his soon-to-be former team-mates as they boarded the coach for a pre-season match.

As he shook hands with the players, coaches and support staff he had known for so long, the Tottenham directors stood by and said nothing. Jennings seemingly took this personally.

On 11 August 1977 Jennings ended his 13-year spell at Tottenham Hotspur and signed for Arsenal in a £45,000 deal.

For Spurs supporters, the idea of a club legend moving to Arsenal was deeply complex. Jennings was never hated. He was barely criticised. Even so, many found it a difficult move to understand. Jennings was surely not without other options, so his choice of club was perplexing.

Eventually the stories of the coach incident, and Jennings's generally shoddy treatment began to leak out. That context, and his subsequent excellent play for the Gunners, ensured that he did what no player before or since has managed to do. He crossed the north London divide and remained popular on both sides. Burkinshaw felt sure that Jennings was ageing and would not be the right choice for Spurs. Instead, Jennings would play 327 times for the Gunners, winning the 1979 FA Cup and keeping his place as first-team keeper at Highbury until 1984. He would return to Tottenham briefly in 1986, making his final appearance for the club in the Football League Super Cup.[22]

---

22 This was a tournament organised as a replacement for the European matches that English clubs missed out on following the Heysel Stadium disaster in 1985.

Part 4: Renaissance

26

From the San Siro to Field Mill

TOTTENHAM HADN'T been in the second tier of English football since 1950, when they had won the division by nine points. The following season they won the club's maiden First Division title.

The ensuing 25 years had changed everything for Tottenham. The heroic exploits of Bill Nicholson's 1960s team in particular had made Spurs a household name for the first time. Now they would be the biggest target in the Second Division. They would face every team's best effort. Everyone would be hoping to claim a famous victory over football royalty.

Tottenham's fans had suffered through years of poor teams. Thrashings by four, five and six goals had become as regular as wins by the same scoreline had previously been. Even the one solid season of the last three had been the result of dour, uninspiring play.

Keith Burkinshaw had proven, even at the cost of relegation, that he was committed to attacking football. That suggested that the drop down to the Second Division promised, if nothing else, a little more fun.

For the players there was pressure. Looking back years later, Glenn Hoddle remembered that there was also a consistent gnawing fear about what would happen to the club if they failed to be promoted back to the top flight at the first time of asking.

The growing finances of the game at the top level had also raised the stakes of failure. A team like Tottenham could ill afford a long stay out of the limelight.

Ninety-eight days after the Leicester City game, Spurs kicked off life in the Second Division against Sheffield United at White Hart Lane.

Seven of the starting XI were the same. There was no Pat Jennings, of course. He was at Portman Road making his debut for Arsenal against Ipswich Town.

Steve Perryman began the campaign in central defence, following a successful experiment in a pre-season match against Leicester. Perryman's energy and quality on the ball gave Spurs the option to build directly from the back.

Keith Osgood scored two penalties, while Chris Jones and John Duncan each added a goal in a 4-2 win over the Blades, the team Tottenham had relegated the season prior to following them down.

A goalless draw against Blackburn Rovers was notable only for being the final starting appearance of Ralph Coates.

Spurs won five of their first seven matches, and sat level at the top of the table, but inconsistency struck in October.

Spurs lost for the first time on a Tuesday night in Hull but they were still second, only one point off the pace. Brighton & Hove Albion, who would play their part in the final drama of the season, were level with Bolton at the top.

Tottenham then smashed Oldham Athletic 5-1 at home and lost 4-1 to Charlton Athletic a week later. Against Oldham, Coates came off the bench for his final minutes as a Tottenham player.

A week after that, Burkinshaw's mother died and so he asked Bill Nicholson to take charge of the match against Bristol Rovers.

Duncan and Jones were injured, so Colin Lee made his debut, just two days after signing from Torquay for £60,000. It turned out to be one of the most spectacular debuts in history for a man who had his leg in plaster just days before making the switch.

Lee, starting alongside Ian Moores in attack, got his first goal after 20 minutes when his strike partner nodded down a Hoddle cross. Five minutes later, Lee scored again as he leapt highest at a corner.

Shortly before half-time, Peter Taylor started a move from inside his own half before arriving in the box to finish it for 3-0. Taylor turned creator after the break, beating his man with a lovely dummy before swinging in a low cross for Moores to scramble home.

Lee added his third, and Tottenham's fifth, from another corner, then Moores made it six when he pounced on a prodded Hoddle pass which had somehow eluded everyone and rolled into the box.

Spurs were playing with utmost confidence now and their seventh goal was a thing of beauty. A sharp passing move put Lee into space down the right, and his cross was as good as Moores's volley.

Lee scored his fourth goal when a Taylor shot was deflected into his path, and who else could have got the ninth but Hoddle, who had been a class above even his impressive team-mates.

Three years after resigning, Nicholson got the spectacular final match in charge that he deserved. A 9-0 victory bookended perfectly the 10-4 win over Everton in his first game all those years before.

The BBC's *Match of the Day* coverage summed the result up by saying, 'You really can't believe it, except that it's happened.' The victory, and the impressive margin, would prove vital by the end of the campaign.

In November, with Spurs on a good run, Burkinshaw gave an interview in which he detailed his philosophy,

'I think that everybody, we all know what we're looking for. The players like playing the way we're playing and I think that it's going to bring us success eventually. We've got to be patient. We all feel this. It's the way we win, sometimes. I feel that we're winning well. Winning the way that I want us to play. I wouldn't be quite so happy if we were winning games and it was a scrappy sort of effort. No, I think that we're starting to play the football that we're all looking for.'

By this point of the season, Spurs were the highest scorers and possessed the second-meanest defence in the division. The fears among players and fans that they might prove unprepared for the rigours of the Second Division appeared to be unfounded.

At the end of the month, Spurs missed the chance to go top as they drew 0-0 with fellow promotion contenders Brighton at White Hart Lane.

A week later, leaders Bolton beat Tottenham 1-0. Another goalless draw, this time against another rival in Southampton, followed seven days further on.

Despite a poor period in which they had picked up just two points and failed to score a goal over three games, Spurs were still second.

Tottenham took off over the Christmas period. They won three out of their next five matches, drawing the other two, as they began an unbeaten league run that wouldn't end until April.

In January, defender Keith Osgood was sold to First Division side Coventry City. In the same month, Tottenham made an unheralded addition to their squad in the form of 22-year-old part-timer Tony Galvin.

Galvin had trials at Huddersfield Town and Leeds United as a teenager, but ended up in the Northern Premier League with Goole Town. He said, 'I was playing one wild, horrible night for Goole and had been told someone was coming to watch. I didn't have a clue who and thought, on a night like this, they probably won't turn up. But Bill Nicholson did.'

Nicholson drove through rain and sleet to get to the match, and the winger impressed – playing in an inch of snow – enough for the legendary former boss to recommend his signing.

Burkinshaw made Galvin an offer but advised him not to take it, instead telling him to finish his teaching certificate as that was more of a 'sure thing' than professional football. Galvin took it, though, and Spurs paid Goole £30,000 for his signature.

The right-footed, left-sided winger admitted later that the move had been unexpected, 'I probably thought Tottenham was a level too high at the time. The culture shock was massive. My first season there, not a lot happened but the second season went well, I started to get into the team.'

Galvin initially joined as a part-timer, on just £50 per week, but would make over 200 appearances for Spurs, breaking into Republic of Ireland team too, despite turning professional at the late age of 22. He even earned a testimonial, played against West Ham in 1987.

There is a pervasive story about Galvin's Ireland career. The legend has it that an official of the Irish FA noticed Galvin playing for Spurs and guessed – because of his family name – that he would be eligible to play for the Republic. Unfortunately, Galvin himself says the story is, 'Rubbish. Absolute rubbish.'

Galvin's actual Irish heritage was on his mother's side. It was Tottenham team-mate Chris Hughton – already playing for Ireland – who figured out that Galvin would be able to join him. The relationship between Hughton and Galvin – Tottenham's left-flank partnership for most of the early 1980s – blossomed almost immediately once the winger became a regular in the first team.

In 1982, Galvin would earn a rare red card after a clash with future Tottenham manager Martin Jol, then playing for West Bromwich Albion.

27

The late wobble

ON 8 April 1978, Spurs faced promotion rivals Bolton Wanderers. Bolton had already knocked them out of the FA Cup after a replay, and had beaten them in the league earlier in the season, so this match loomed particularly large.

White Hart Lane was packed. Fans thought it as full that day as any other they could remember. On the same afternoon Arsenal were playing an FA Cup semi-final at Stamford Bridge, yet Spurs drew a bigger crowd.

The atmosphere in north London was boiling. It felt more like a cup final or big European night than a late-season league match.

Don McAllister – against his former club – scored the only goal of the game to give his new team what seemed a particularly important victory. At full time Tottenham were two points clear at the top with four games to go. But that was when the problems began.

A week later, Spurs travelled to Alan Mullery's Brighton & Hove Albion. The hosts were leading the chasing pack of potential promotion sides, and a defeat against Tottenham would have more or less ended their hopes.

In the reverse fixture the previous November, Brighton had become the first team that season to take a point at White Hart Lane in what was the first league meeting between the two clubs. John Duncan, absent again with injury since March, returned for the match, although before the kick-off police battled fans trying to scale the fences at the Goldstone Ground. Scalpers were selling tickets for 25 times their face value.

Fifteen minutes in, the referee called a halt as fans spilled on to the pitch to avoid the brawling in the stands. The teams were taken off for 14 minutes before order was restored and the match could resume.

When it did, Brighton took control with two quick goals. Chris Jones pulled one back but substitute Eric Potts sealed a 3-1 victory in the second half. Tottenham still held top spot on goal difference, but Southampton and Bolton had pulled level with their 53 points.

Fifty-one people were arrested and 85 treated for injuries after the clashes, with 20 of those having to be hospitalised. The FA responded to the serious – even by the standards of the time – violence by ordering Brighton to install perimeter fencing around their pitch.

By mid-April Sunderland's promotion hopes had already faded. Thirteen points off the top, and with a manager who would not see out the year – Jimmy Adamson, who had captained Burnley in the 1962 FA Cup Final against Tottenham – the Mackems, as they were then, should not have been too much for Spurs.

Tottenham were unbeaten at home, with a place in the First Division at stake, and Peter Taylor scored after 25 seconds but nothing went right from there.

Gerry Armstrong gifted Sunderland their equaliser before Bob Lee added two more. Duncan pulled one back but Sunderland keeper Barry Siddall shone to seal the win.

Only once before that season had Tottenham failed to respond to a league defeat with victory in their next match. They hadn't lost back-to-back games in over a year. Now, though, with promotion there for the taking, Keith Burkinshaw's side were stuttering.

The *Daily Mirror* reported that abject depression had set in among Spurs fans, with the question of whether they would stay up the next season now replaced by whether they would go up at all. Spurs had surrendered top spot as Southampton and Bolton kept winning. They had now slipped to third and sat just a point above Brighton.

First and fourth in the Second Division were separated by just three points with two games to go. No one else could catch the leaders and it was going to be three of the top four to earn promotion. One was going to miss out.

Already relegated Hull City were Tottenham's next opponent, and once again they found a theoretically unmotivated team playing highly motivated football. Defending as though they could somehow reverse their relegation if only they could keep Spurs at bay, Hull resisted until the 81st minute. Then, from Tottenham's 28th corner of the match, controversy struck.

Hull keeper Eddie Blackburn came and claimed Glenn Hoddle's corner easily enough but he was knocked down and dropped the ball. Captain Steve Perryman pounced to put away the loose ball and White Hart Lane erupted. A full-scale pitch invasion was barely avoided as police dragged celebrating fans away from the Spurs players.

All the while, the Hull players were protesting at the apparently blatant foul on their goalkeeper. Hull manager Ken Houghton was 'sick' over the decision, calling it 'one of the most diabolical decisions I've ever seen'.

Blackburn had played magnificently, making 'at least six' brilliant saves. Duncan admitted after the match that it was he who had knocked Blackburn down. After a frustrating game in which he had played poorly, Duncan decided, 'I'm just going to go for it as hard as I can. I just took my chance that it wouldn't be given; it was a free kick.'

Much later, Perryman was still puzzled by the fervour with which Hull played to stop Spurs.

'I think I found out afterwards that there was some extra meaning in the game for them as well. I'm not suggesting a bribe or anything, but we noted to each other afterwards, Christ, for a team that was playing out the season, they didn't half have a go.'

After the match, the fans invaded the pitch and stayed, dancing and singing, for half an hour. When they finally cleared out, the playing surface had been hacked to pieces. Thousands of tiny squares of turf were carried off as souvenirs of a promotion almost certainly won.

The same night, Bolton were officially promoted. Two places in the 1978/79 First Division remained up for grabs with one match remaining. Southampton and Brighton had won to keep pace with Spurs, and the final day would decide their fate.

Mullery's Brighton had finished the season in excellent form, winning six of their final eight to roar into promotion contention. Spurs had won just twice in as many matches. Brighton might have been favourites to snatch the final promotion place, except that Spurs' remaining fixture was against Southampton.

The Saints were assured of promotion if they avoided defeat, a result which would also see Tottenham promoted unless Brighton could win by 11 goals. A point was all Spurs would need to deny Brighton and return to the top flight, although before the match, Burkinshaw stressed that he would never tell his players to abandon the attacking style that had made them the division's top scorers.

Saturday, 29 April 1978 dawned cold. Temperatures had been down near freezing overnight. Spurs fans piled into trains and on to coaches as they headed towards the south coast and a nerve-wracking 90 minutes.

Southampton midfielder Alan Ball is rumoured to have told Tottenham players before the match that both sides needed a point and that nobody should rock the boat.

Before the game, even Brighton's manager essentially admitted he wanted to see his old club promoted. Mullery said, 'I have to take the view that the game generally will be the loser if Spurs fail.'

John Pratt escaped what appeared to be a handball in the box in the first half, and Southampton soon hit the post. Hoddle then played in Taylor who tried for a penalty with a rather unimpressive dive, but the match remained goalless at half-time.

Late in the match, a rumour went around the Tottenham fans that Brighton were losing. Cheers went up, but the story was snuffed out just as quickly when fans with radios reported that Brighton were in fact 2-1 up against Blackpool.

Neither Tottenham nor their hosts had managed a shot on target as the match meandered towards full time.

In the final minute, Tony Funnell – who had scored nine goals in 14 appearances that season – hit the post for a second time but the ball was cleared away and Spurs survived.

The game finished goalless and Spurs held on for the point that they needed. The nightmare scenario of a prolonged stay in the Second Division – a trap which has caught many great clubs before and since – had been avoided. Promotion was secured on goal difference as the 9-0 win over Bristol Rovers proved decisive.

Southampton had spent £6,000 to erect a new fence specifically to stop Tottenham fans launching a second pitch invasion in as many matches. It was kicked to pieces at half-time, but the extra police laid on for the same reason had the desired effect until full time when thousands of supporters from both sides spilled on to the pitch to celebrate promotion.

A line of police with dogs kept them well apart. Some bottles were thrown back and forth, but nothing more dramatic occurred.

Perryman was a little sheepish in the post-match celebrations, saying, 'It could have been a real travesty if we had not made it. There was a lot of pressure on us. It's amazing how we have given goals away late in the season.'

'After last Saturday's home defeat by Sunderland I began to wonder whether it was all worth it. But these players have shown great character and strength,' said Burkinshaw. He admitted that he had 'died a thousand deaths' that day and during the late-season wobble.

Stories about Southampton against Spurs on the final day of the 1977/78 season have grown in the telling over the years. Did Keith Burkinshaw and Lawrie McMenemy really walk out of the tunnel arm-in-arm as so many have said? They certainly shook hands but no contemporary reports back up that more titillating version.

Did Southampton really stop passing the ball to Alan Ball after he seemed to be trying too hard to win the match? Did Southampton decide that winning, and going for the title, was not worth the riot it might provoke from angry Spurs fans and play for a draw instead?

The truth about these rumours may never be fully known, but certainly no player involved has ever admitted to 'taking it easy'.

Many of these stories hold particular currency among Brighton supporters. Their team was, of course, the victim of the envisioned conspiracy.

At full time at the Goldstone Ground, after Brighton had beaten Blackpool only to fall short of promotion, Mullery grabbed a microphone and promised his supporters that his team would be promoted the next year.

Twelve months later Mullery was proven right as Brighton joined Spurs and Southampton in the First Division.

In the end, the Second Division sojourn had been enjoyable for Tottenham fans. They had visited new grounds, and actually had the opportunity to see their team win some games. Only towards the end, as the victories suddenly dried up, did a sense of dread return.

For the team, and manager too, it had also been a positive experience. Burkinshaw had had the opportunity to establish his attacking philosophy – his team scored 83 goals, 13 more than the next best attack – against relatively weaker opposition, while discovering Perryman's suitability for his new role in defence.

Perryman, already Burkinshaw's captain, became his confidant. The manager recalled years later, 'Every Sunday we'd talk for a couple of hours on the phone about what had happened the previous week, what we were going to do the following week. I knew that when he went on the field, he was carrying on what I believed in.'

Their relationship blossomed that season, as Spurs were given the time and space to really play the attacking football in which Burkinshaw believed.

The captain was vital in the re-establishing of the 'Tottenham way' of playing. Burkinshaw knew he had a dependable player who could be his on-field coach, 'Anything that I wanted to do on the field, he would be the one that carried it on there.'

Although a drastically different kind of player, Perryman became to Burkinshaw what Danny Blanchflower had been to Bill Nicholson. Their connection would prove central to all that the team would achieve.

The drop to the Second Division had also given Glenn Hoddle the perfect opportunity to shine. He had played almost every game. Thriving with the slower pace of the second tier, he scored 13 goals and secured his position as one of England's finest emerging talents.

28

Spurs scoop the world

THEIR MISSION accomplished, Tottenham would face a new challenge back in the First Division.

Admittedly, the gap between divisions was not yet as great as it would become in later years. Only three teams – Luton Town and Carlisle in 1975 and Sunderland in 1977 – had been relegated immediately after promotion since the shift to three up and three down after the 1973/74 season. Nevertheless, Tottenham would need reinforcements if they were to make an impact back among England's elite.

Thirty-two days after the Southampton match, the World Cup kicked off.

England had missed qualification, so too the European champions Czechoslovakia. France and Spain ended 12-year absences by qualifying but all attention was on the hosts, Argentina, and the favourites, the Johan Cruyff-less Netherlands.

Argentina qualified for the final with a controversial 6-0 win over Peru. The Dutch beat Italy to secure their own place in the showpiece, where Mario Kempes scored twice as the South Americans won 3-1 after extra time.

A few days after the final, Bill Nicholson received a phone call from Harry Haslam, the manager of Sheffield United. Oscar Arce, an Argentinian on his staff, had told him that two of the World Cup-winning squad – Ricardo Villa and Osvaldo Ardiles – wanted to come to England.

However, they would only join a 'top' club and the fee was expected to be around £400,000 – money that the Blades did not have.

Nicholson had seen Ardiles during the World Cup and considered him an obvious improvement to Spurs' squad. Villa, who had played sparingly in the tournament, was a lesser known quantity.

Former Argentina captain Antonio Rattín – who had been sent off against England during the 1966 World Cup – had personally recommended Villa. It emerged that he would be handling negotiations with Racing and Huracán, the respective clubs of Villa and Ardiles.

Nicholson told Keith Burkinshaw, and both men were immediately excited at the prospect. Burkinshaw went to the board that day. Chairman Sidney Wale was willing to fund a potential deal so talks began.

Arsenal boss Terry Neill was also aware of the negotiations and considering a bid, while Manchester City had dropped out of contention due to the size of the fee.

Burkinshaw flew to Buenos Aires to speak to the players. There is a pervasive rumour that Ardiles and Villa were never explicitly told that they were joining a club which had played its most recent season in the English Second Division until well after they signed.

Rattín met the party at the airport in Buenos Aires and his gentility surprised the Englishmen, who had been fed the notion of the Argentinian as a wild and violent man following his 1966 dismissal.

Shortly after arriving, the Spurs group learned that Arsenal – who didn't want any non-English players – had dropped out, leaving them free to move for the pair.

Although Burkinshaw didn't realise before arriving, it became clear that the deal was a package. It was both players or neither. The fee for Ardiles was £350,000, easily Tottenham's transfer record, but well short of the British record. Earlier in the summer Manchester United had bought Leeds United's Scottish centre-back Gordon McQueen for a fee reported to be between £500,000 and £950,000 depending on the source, and along with McQueen's Scotland and Leeds team-mate Joe Jordan for over £300,000.

There were concerns that Spurs may not have had the capacity to pay, however, so Wale had to increase the club's bank overdraft on the basis of assumed increased ticket sales.

With the fee agreed, it was the players' turn. A joke emerged from the apparent swiftness with which they signed their contracts. Ardiles agreed terms in 20 minutes; Villa took much longer, about three quarters of an hour.

With the Argentinian economy struggling from the consequences of decades of dictatorial rule, its football clubs were desperate for liquid currency. The fee was paid – in Canadian dollars due to the specific demands on the Argentinian side – and the deal was done.

The impact of the signing was immense. For Tottenham's fans, it ignited a sense of optimism and swept away any fears that their return to the top flight would be short-lived. Instead, the dream of a title challenge began to carry some of the more optimistic supporters away.

While there was near uniform happiness in England, it was more complex on the Argentinian side of the deal. After Rattín had been sent off during England's 1-0 win over Argentina in the quarter-finals of the World Cup in 1966, Alf Ramsey declared that the Argentinians had 'played like animals'. It became an infamous line in Argentina, stoking an already smouldering anti-British feeling.

While the Falkland Islands wouldn't become internationally known until 1982, in 1978 they were already part of a minor diplomatic crisis. The Argentinian government had removed its ambassador from London over both the disputed islands and a further border issue. The Beagle Channel, which separates Chile and Argentina at the southernmost point of South America, contains several islands which both countries claimed.

An ongoing attempt at international arbitration (lasting from 1971 to 1977) had by now failed and Argentina and Chile were on the brink of war. The role of the British crown as arbitrator in this conflict had led the Argentinian junta to blame Britain for the crisis.

The combination of Ramsey's 'animals' quote, the Beagle Channel crisis and the still unresolved issue of the Falklands, meant there was a strong vein of anti-British feeling among the Argentinian people. Consequently, when Don Revie's England visited Argentina on a tour in 1977, the team were abused, the anthem booed and anti-British banners were unfurled at matches.

Ardiles had good reason to fear that the English crowd might prove equally hostile to the arrival of two Argentinians. Then there were concerns at Tottenham that the players' union back in England might veto the deal. The PFA did step in, attempting to block the signings on the grounds that Ardiles and Villa would put two English players out of jobs. England manager Ron Greenwood made the opposite argument, suggesting that the presence of accomplished international players could only raise the standard of the British game.

The issue was trending towards a damaging stalemate until it emerged that Southampton had already signed Yugoslavian Ivan Golac from FK Partizan, and the PFA had failed to block the deal, undercutting their position against Ardiles and Villa.

That hurdle cleared, the players next had to undergo medical examinations. Though a transfer medical is usually a simple formality, there was yet another wrinkle to the deal as

Ardiles had a fractured toe, which meant he could neither run, nor kick a ball, but he had been reluctant to disclose anything that might have jeopardised the move.

He fretted throughout the examination, fearful that the doctors would spot the injury and cancel the deal, but he was relieved when he saw his x-rays. The medical staff had only taken images of his legs down to the ankle, missing the injury.

Ardiles's Argentinian doctor had promised him that the injury would heal without surgery, and it eventually did so in time for him to join Spurs' pre-season preparations.

After completing the medical exams, the players returned to Argentina for a belated post-World Cup holiday.

Upon their return, Burkinshaw had no doubts about their ability to adjust to the English league – Argentinian football has never been delicate – but he did fear that life in England might not suit them.

In order to help ensure their successful transition to England, Burkinshaw rented a single large house in Chigwell. It was deliberately big enough for both players as well as their families to move in, providing the support network that the manager suspected would be vital.

In more modern times, a player transferred in from an exotic league is usually well supported by the club. They have to protect their investment, after all. But in 1978, Tottenham were breaking new ground and coming up with these ideas on the fly.

Ardiles's pregnant wife had remained in Argentina for the birth of his son, Pablo. He called her three times a day until he got a £200 phone bill.

The success of the Argentinian duo owes much to the enthusiasm with which Peter Taylor took to his role as their 'minder'. Seeing that their English was not yet perfect, Taylor bought an English-Spanish dictionary to help and introduced them to his friends away from football.

Villa's first introduction to the Tottenham players was to beat them at a frame of snooker while on a training camp at Zeist.

Their debuts came in a pre-season match against Royal Antwerp on 8 August. The 200 Spurs fans in attendance welcomed the new players to the pitch with a homemade ticker tape parade – brought to the ground by fans carrying plastic carrier bags stuffed with torn up paper – as Ardiles appeared in the first half, while Villa played for 90 minutes.

Villa came close to a debut goal, but Ian Moores's two headers plus a Glenn Hoddle penalty gave Spurs a 3-1 win.

John Duncan had been considered certain to leave over the summer. In July, newspaper reports claimed the Scottish striker was set to return north of the border, with a £100,000 transfer to Motherwell apparently agreed, but the deal never went through.

Twenty-seven-year-old centre-back John Lacy was signed from Fulham for £200,000. Lacy would be an ever-present alongside Holmes and McAllister in the Spurs defence.

Ralph Coates was given a free transfer to join Leyton Orient after making just one league appearance in the promotion-winning season. Coates had joined Spurs at the tail end of their glory years, and scored the winner to earn what was at that time their most recent trophy.

29

It's a long way to the top

TOTTENHAM'S FIRST opponents of 1978/79 were the reigning First Division champions and soon-to-be European Cup winners Nottingham Forest.

This was Brian Clough's historic side, still on the rise. They had been promoted from the Second Division in 1977, and won the top-flight title at their first attempt.

The arrival of Ossie Ardiles and Ricardo Villa had sparked a betting plunge on Tottenham to match Forest in winning the league in their first year back up, and the trip to the City Ground would provide an immediate test of those pretensions.

Ardiles suffered a slight strain in the build-up to the match and his participation was briefly in doubt, but ultimately he and Villa both started, and so too did fellow new signing John Lacy. John Gorman made his first appearance in 18 months. Gorman had missed the entire promotion campaign with injury, but Burkinshaw put him straight back into the team.

The supporters travelling up to Nottingham were as full of hope and expectation as could be. There is blind optimism associated with the first match of any season, but 1978 was special. Tottenham had not only returned to the First Division, they had done it playing attacking football. Now they faced a glamour opening against the champions and had their exotic new stars in the starting line-up.

The kick-off was delayed for 15 minutes while hooligans fought on the pitch. Once things finally got underway the atmosphere was electric.

From their first touches, Ardiles and Villa gave a sense of what was to come. Their skill, their control, their alien touches; it all sparked the crowd's excitement.

Martin O'Neill gave the champions the lead after John Robertson's early cross. O'Neill's first shot was blocked but he scored on the follow-up.

Spurs produced a team move to respond in the 25th minute. Gorman played Ian Moores into space down the left. Moores crossed early to Villa who was one-on-one with Peter Shilton.

Villa dummied to shoot, ducked left to pass Shilton and rolled it into the empty net. There was elation among the players and ecstasy for the fans who had endured some wretched years.

The match finished as a draw, and Tottenham came away delighted with their start. To have faced down the champions, with star signings Villa and Ardiles shining, was to suggest that Spurs would be right at home in the top division.

Four days later, it was time for the Argentinians to experience a home game with a First Division match scheduled at White Hart Lane for the first time in 466 days.

The perfect beginning against Forest had seemed too good to be true, and of course, it was.

Tottenham fans welcomed the arrival of their two new Argentinian stars by staging another South American-style ticker-tape parade. This time, thousands of fans joined in and the pitch was blanketed in confetti.

For a moment at least, a corner of north London was transformed. White Hart Lane felt more like La Bombonera or El Monumental.

Once the match got under way, the party atmosphere soon disappeared. Aston Villa were a strong side, building towards a league title in 1981 and a famous European Cup win in 1982. They proved far too good for Spurs.

One of Ardiles's first touches at White Hart Lane was a back-heel which missed its intended target and almost gave team-mate Villa an early goal.

The visitors did open the scoring after 35 minutes, soon adding a second. Ardiles won a penalty, which was duly converted by Hoddle, on the hour to keep Spurs in it, but two quick goals made it 4-1; a sobering reversal after the encouraging performance against Forest. To make things worse, Peter Taylor limped off late with an ankle injury.

Where Forest had sought an open game, giving Tottenham space to play, Villa defended aggressively.

Steve Perryman admitted afterwards that the occasion had gotten to his players, 'The whole team felt a bit nervous and not just Ardiles and Villa.' He conceded that the Argentinians were still something of an 'experiment' but insisted that they would find their feet, and it would 'pay off in the long run'.

Burkinshaw agreed, saying, 'The Argentinians did not play as well as they have done, especially Villa. Tonight was a lesson for these two lads. They probably know what they are up against in English football.'

The manager's comments today read like cliche, but he was possibly the first person to ever deploy the notion of being 'welcomed' to the English league.

Burkinshaw also admitted that his team needed to adapt to the speed of First Division football, saying, 'Villa denied us space better than any team last season.'

Ardiles admitted that he was struggling with Burkinshaw's tactical instructions. He found himself limited by the specific role he had been assigned, and thus unable to play with the freedom to which he was accustomed.

Three days later, Tottenham faced the prospect of a London derby against Chelsea. It was the first meeting between the two clubs since the famous night in 1975 when Tottenham sent the Blues down to the Second Division.

All police leave was cancelled ahead of the match, with more than 300 officers posted around White Hart Lane. Chelsea fans had wrought havoc throughout the previous season, while Spurs had seen plenty of trouble themselves. The explosive rivalry sparked fears of a major outbreak of violence on the terraces.

In their previous league game, a win against Wolverhampton Wanderers, Blues fans stormed the North Bank at Molineux. Infamously led by a one-armed man, Chelsea supporters slipped in through the open exit gates late in the match, causing chaos and making headlines.

The fixture got under way and after just nine minutes came the first goal to truly mark Tottenham's new era. Ardiles dribbled down the line and passed to Villa who back-heeled it for John Duncan to score in his first appearance of the season.

Chants of 'viva, viva' – Spurs fans' response to the brilliance of their new stars – echoed around the ground, and twice Ardiles went close to scoring, both times set up by Duncan.

Chelsea equalised quickly, robbing Glenn Hoddle as he dawdled on the ball, but Ardiles and Villa combined again to restore Tottenham's lead, setting up Gerry Armstrong to score.

The Blues got back level again before Villa danced past three defenders and fizzed a shot inches wide of the post. Both keepers were then busy in the final minutes but it finished a 2-2 draw.

Chelsea defender Steve Wicks said after the match, 'Ardiles could cost Spurs a lot of goals. He doesn't get back too quickly. The top teams might just murder Tottenham.'

On the terraces, the anticipated violence did indeed come to pass. Forty-one people were arrested in the stadium but the greatest violence came after the match, in an ugly incident at

Seven Sisters railway station. There, six fans and two police were injured in a long-remembered battle.

Spurs still hadn't won a game, and next up was a trip to Anfield to face a Liverpool side at their absolute peak. They were two-time defending European champions and in the middle of a relentless spell of four league titles in five seasons. They had won their opening three matches, scoring nine and conceding two.

Kenny Dalglish, Alan Hansen and former Tottenham midfielder Graeme Souness had all been added to Liverpool's already mighty team in the previous six months.

Spurs still had not won at Anfield since March 1912 and there was little reason to think that streak would end in 1978.

In the opening minutes, Villa dribbled through midfield and stabbed a pass in behind Liverpool's high defensive line. Duncan beat the offside trap and raced towards the box without a defender in sight. With Hoddle and Villa unmarked at the top of the box, Duncan tried to round Ray Clemence, but the Liverpool keeper bravely dived at his feet to snuff out a huge early chance.

Moments later, Dalglish used the pace of a mishit shot to spin Steve Perryman just inside the Spurs box before rolling his shot under the sprawling Barry Daines.

Five minutes later Daines did well to deny Steve Heighway's rocketing free kick, but he could do nothing when Dalglish unleashed from distance to double Liverpool's lead.

Ray Kennedy headed in Liverpool's third after 28 minutes and the gulf in class, already apparent, seemed to yawn ever wider.

A diving save from Daines denied Jimmy Case's long-distance attempt as Spurs survived the remainder of the first period, lucky to only trail 3-0 at the break.

After half-time, things somehow got worse. David Johnson rifled home a loose ball that Tottenham's defence had seemingly decided not to clear in the 48th minute. Johnson made it 5-0 by rolling a shot between Daines's legs.

Duncan took away Liverpool's chance for a sixth goal with a sensational bicycle-kick clearance off his own line, but gave it right back when he conceded a penalty moments later. Daines actually saved the spot-kick but the referee, taking absolutely no mercy, ordered it to be retaken and Phil Neal converted at the second attempt.

Spurs, pushing forward to try to reduce the scoreline, were cut apart by a Liverpool counter which ended with a flying Terry McDermott header which made it 7-0.

The *Match of the Day* coverage summed things up nicely, saying, 'Liverpool have absolutely slaughtered Spurs.'

It was Tottenham's new record league defeat. Four matches into the season they were 21st with a -10 goal difference. Only Queens Park Rangers – just one point behind – kept Burkinshaw's team off the bottom.

30

Green shoots

FOLLOWING THE Liverpool debacle, Swansea City – a third tier-team which had just been promoted from the Fourth Division the previous season – knocked Spurs out of the League Cup.

In response to these consecutive humiliations, Keith Burkinshaw dropped five starters. Glenn Hoddle, Terry Naylor, Gerry Armstrong, Neil McNab and John Duncan were all left out for the following match, the visit of Bristol City. Tottenham finally got a win; a David Rodgers own goal was the difference in a tight affair at White Hart Lane.

Next, Spurs went to Leeds and won again. Peter Taylor scored a brilliant opener, robbing the ball in midfield and leaving Leeds' defence in his wake as he raced off to score.

Spurs got caught trying to play out from the back in the second half and Leeds equalised, but with time running out Ossie Ardiles unleashed a vicious shot from the edge of the area. His shot was saved, but Colin Lee pounced on the loose ball to give Spurs victory.

Duncan and McNab would never play for Tottenham again. McNab was furious at his benching, telling the press, 'I feel I've been kicked in the teeth.' The Scottish utility man had dovetailed with Hoddle effectively throughout the promotion campaign, and was rewarded with a four-year contract that summer, but Burkinshaw's mind was not to be changed.

McNab had been signed for £40,000 from Scottish amateurs Greenock Morton as a 16-year-old by Bill Nicholson, having to wait a year before he could make his debut because of regulations prohibiting youth players playing men's football. Impressing immediately, comparisons had been made to Tottenham legend John White.

He had struggled for game time under Terry Neill but been ever-present in the Second Division season. Now, with Burkinshaw looking to both make necessary changes and a point, he was sold to Bolton Wanderers for £250,000. The Trotters had been chasing McNab since the end of the previous season, and finally got their man.

Derby County made a £150,000 offer for Duncan, and Spurs accepted it. Duncan had scored 62 goals in four years at the club. His goals had kept Tottenham up in 1975, and his absence two years later had been a huge factor in their relegation. Duncan admitted later that he regretted the departure, saying it was probably a short-sighted response to no longer being a guaranteed starter.

He began well at his new club, scoring after seven minutes on debut. But he would only score 11 more in three seasons at the Baseball Ground and he suffered his second relegation in four years when Derby dropped into the Second Division the following season.

Next, striker Ian Moores was sold to Leyton Orient for £80,000.

After Tottenham lost again, 2-0 away at Manchester City, Ricky Villa was dropped to substitute duty. He spent the next six matches on the bench, admittedly being brought on in each one, and felt compelled to play for the reserves against Oxford in December just to get 90 minutes.

That coincided with a run of improved results. Draws against Coventry, Derby and Norwich, and wins over West Bromwich Albion, Derby and Bolton, took Spurs into the top half of the table. They still had a -6 goal difference but they had won more games than they had lost and gradually began to look like a solid team.

Burkinshaw was stubbornly dedicated to playing the same attacking football that he had installed in the Second Division, but he wasn't foolish. He had tweaked the approach and Spurs were no longer playing quite so open.

Burkinshaw would admit later that his all-out attacking style was perhaps not the best way to win, but believed that it was what the fans deserved to watch.

The strong run continued until a 3-1 home defeat against Forest broke the unbeaten streak, but Spurs responded well. They won three of their next four, over Chelsea, Wolves and Ipswich, also earning a creditable 0-0 draw against Liverpool, and reached December in eighth place.

In mid-December, Luton Town goalkeeper Milija Aleksic was signed for £100,000. Barry Daines was injured, so Spurs had been playing 20-year-old Mark Kendall.

Aleksic had been dropped by Luton over a wage dispute, and started off life at Tottenham in the reserves as Burkinshaw was reluctant to leave out Kendall, but the Englishman was not unhappy. Aleksic said, 'I know I will have to wait for a first team chance, but I'm certain I'll get a fair crack of the whip.'

On 23 December, Pat Jennings returned to White Hart Lane in the colours of Arsenal for the first time. John Motson labelled the match a 'Cockney Cup Final at Christmas'.

Two other former Spurs players started for Arsenal – Willie Young and Steve Walford – and they were still managed by Terry Neill.

Arsenal were fourth in the league but only three points ahead of Spurs. The home fans might have been forgiven for thinking that the sight of the Northern Irish giant with a cannon over his heart was as bad as things could be but instead, Arsenal handed their north London rivals a humiliation.

The Gunners scored inside the first minute when a cautious back-pass from John Pratt backfired spectacularly. Alan Sunderland beat the flat-footed John Lacey and smashed his shot past Kendall for the early lead.

Colin Lee left Willie Young flailing and could have played in Peter Taylor for the equaliser but took on the shot from a difficult angle, squandering the golden chance.

Sunderland doubled Arsenal's lead when he shot right through Kendall just before half-time. A diving Frank Stapleton header made it 3-0 on the hour, and Liam Brady added a fourth with a deflected shot three minutes later.

Sunderland completed both his hat-trick and Tottenham's misery in the 82nd minute, and it could have been even worse had Stapleton not hit the woodwork in added time.

Liam Brady, not yet at the height of his powers, was magnificent in midfield. The Irishman was probably the best player on the pitch despite Sunderland scoring three goals.

It had not been nearly as comprehensive a hammering as Spurs had suffered at Anfield, but a derby defeat of that magnitude was another heavy blow for Burkinshaw to absorb.

On Boxing Day, Spurs picked up a 2-2 draw against Queens Park Rangers, and four days later another point was won against Everton at Goodison Park.

By January Spurs were comfortably mid-table, and far from relegation danger. It seemed as though the minimum goal for the season – survival – was well in hand.

Britain was caught in the vice of the so-called 'Winter of Discontent', another turbulent period for the economy characterised by strikes, inflation and the coldest temperatures since the Great Freeze of 1963.

Despite the less-than-ideal economic conditions, Spurs' incomes had reached new heights. They had recorded a turnover of £1.4m in 1979, enough to help Burkinshaw improve his team and target real success.

Tottenham's wealth, and that of football generally, had already moved into the strange position it has held ever since of being somewhat impervious to economic trends. In Bill Nicholson's era, general economic troubles meant clubs would have to tighten their belts, but this was becoming less and less the case.

Within five years Tottenham would be earning over £5m per year despite ongoing issues with the British economy as a whole. Football was becoming untethered from reality.

After a six-match run without a win, Burkinshaw took drastic action in February. Aleksic, Pratt, Lee and Jones were all dropped with Stuart Beavon and Tony Galvin handed their debuts against Manchester City, but sadly the gamble did not pay off. Spurs were hammered 3-0, completely shown up tactically and the debutants were notable for being 'out of their depth'.

In the same month, Tottenham signed Aston Villa full-back Gordon Smith for £150,000. Smith had been transfer-listed at his own request following a period out of the first team. Burkinshaw had Smith scouted multiple times, but the deal almost fell through.

After Spurs and Villa had agreed a fee, Smith was due to travel to White Hart Lane to discuss terms, but he never arrived.

Eventually it emerged that Smith had broken down somewhere on the M1. The transfer, once completed, took Tottenham's spending for the season past £1m.

While Burkinshaw had money to spend, the board insisted that the club finish every season with a positive balance sheet. Aleksic, Smith, Lacy and the Argentinians had been added, but Duncan, McNab, Moores, Coates and a handful of academy players went the other way.

Spurs' FA Cup campaign began in mid-January against Northern Premier League side Altrincham. Tottenham hadn't won a single FA Cup match since 1973, and the prospect of a fifth-tier club visiting White Hart Lane gave hope that the streak would finally be ended.

With nationwide petrol shortages caused by striking oil tanker drivers – part of the ongoing economic tremors striking the country – the match was initially postponed and moved to a Wednesday.

Spurs put out a strong team, with Ossie Ardiles and Ricardo Villa starting alongside Steve Perryman and Peter Taylor, but Altrincham had been FA Trophy finalists the season before and would apply for Football League membership at the end of the campaign, although they were unsuccessful. They would not be the soft touch that many anticipated.

The match started well enough when Taylor scored a penalty, but Altrincham equalised through Jeff Johnson to stun the home crowd and earn a replay.

Altrincham's home ground was not able to host the return match, so it was held at Manchester City's Maine Road instead. Lee – who had been playing more as a back-up full-back than a striker – scored a hat-trick in a 3-0 win. It was his final contribution before being sold to Chelsea a few days later for £225,000. He had scored twice against the bottom-of-the-table Blues in November.

Chelsea would be relegated that season, continuing a yo-yo existence begun back in 1975 when they had gone down at Tottenham's hand. Lee became a key player in the following campaign and stayed at Stamford Bridge for eight years.

Second Division side Wrexham were Spurs' next opponents in the FA Cup. The Robins had been promoted the previous season as Third Division champions, and won the Welsh Cup. Like Altrincham they could not be underestimated, and like Altrincham they earned a replay, drawing 3-3 at White Hart Lane.

The replay proved trickier for Spurs to navigate this time. Chris Jones scored after eight minutes, but Wrexham equalised just before the end to force extra time. Dixie McNeil scored first in the additional half an hour but Jones scored twice in 13 minutes to turn things around and give Spurs victory.

It was another Second Division side, Oldham Athletic, in the fifth round. This time Tottenham advanced with a minimum of fuss as Perryman scored the only goal at Boundary Park to earn a place in the last eight.

Tottenham hadn't reached the quarter-final of the FA Cup since 1972. They hadn't gone further than that since last winning the trophy in 1967.

White Hart Lane was heaving with a crowd of well over 50,000 on 10 March with Manchester United the visitors. Jones had the ball in the net early, but the goal was ruled out for a foul on United goalkeeper Gary Bailey. Then Don McAllister hit the post with a header, and Glenn Hoddle was humming, while Ardiles was everywhere linking the play.

Spurs were dominating and United had barely crossed halfway when Jones won a foul deep in their territory. Perryman sent it in and Ardiles – completely unmarked – headed Tottenham into the lead.

Ardiles soon won another foul and Jones escaped his marker to smash his shot towards goal, but Bailey got a touch and turned it wide. Not long afterwards, a quick throw found Ardiles who knocked the ball past his man and was hacked down. No penalty was given and the whistle shortly blew for half time.

Already a cold day, it began to rain and the White Hart Lane pitch began to loosen up underfoot. Spurs had had all the play but gradually began to lose control in the second half. United finally mounted their first meaningful attack but Steve Coppell scuffed his shot when through on goal.

At the other end, after Kendall recovered the ball to restart play, a large bottle was thrown in his direction from the United fans. Kendall was suddenly the busier of the two keepers. If not under siege, the Tottenham goal was certainly under pressure. He pushed a Coppell shot wide, but Welsh midfielder Mickey Thomas bundled in an equaliser from the ensuing corner almost exactly on the hour mark.

Furious Spurs appeals for another penalty were denied when Jones and Villa were both knocked down in the United box. It was Villa's last contribution as he was replaced by Taylor.

Perryman almost gave United a winner with a blind back-pass intercepted by Coppell, before Taylor had a great chance of his own.

The match was completely open now and each side took its turn to pile forward but neither could find the winner.

Tottenham were outmatched in the replay, however. Joe Jordan scored a looping header after just ten minutes and Sammy McIlroy pounced on hesitant Spurs defending to snatch a killer second on the hour.

Defeat at Old Trafford meant Tottenham's trophy drought would extend to at least seven years, but they had proven they could at least contend for cups again.

Burkinshaw's side were growing together, and with a little more luck in the home draw they could easily have advanced to the semi-final.

As it was, United moved on and beat Liverpool in a replay before losing to Terry Neill's Arsenal in the final at Wembley.

A 3-2 win at Aston Villa in March put Spurs six wins clear of the drop zone, but with safety secured and no trophies left to play for, their form fell off sharply.

They drew their next match, at home to Southampton, before losing their next four straight. The last of that run was another north London derby – this time 1-0 – with the sole positive being the debut of Paul Miller.

Miller had joined Spurs as an apprentice in 1976. He went to Norwegian club Skeid on loan in 1977/78 where he was voted the league's best foreign player. Miller would be in and out of the first team for most of the rest 1978/79 but soon became a fixture until his departure in 1987 – nearly 300 games later.

Spurs went on a run of two months without a win and had slipped down to 16th by the start of May. They were already safe by some distance, but the barren run had stripped some of the varnish off a fine first season back in the top flight.

They signed off with victories over Bolton Wanderers and West Bromwich Albion, moving up to their final finishing position of 11th.

Eighteen-year-old striker Mark Falco scored on his debut against Bolton. Falco was the latest academy graduate to emerge and join the first team squad, who had been raised under the tutelage of Peter Shreeves.

Burkinshaw had achieved the initial objective of keeping Tottenham in the First Division, and there were promising signs that his star signings had begun to find their feet in English football.

A week before Falco's debut, Margaret Thatcher's Conservative party were elected to government. The rise of the Conservatives would define the 1980s. Economic liberalisation policies would allow Spurs to become the first club to be listed on the stock exchange, and then steer into financial disaster.

The election saw the largest swing since the end of the Second World War. The National Front, previously a consideration if not a major factor, were swallowed up by Conservative gains. They had lost more than half of their voters, most of whom swung to Thatcher's side.

31

Neither here nor there

DAYS BEFORE the 1979/80 season began, Tottenham signed Coventry City and Wales captain Terry Yorath for £300,000. The 29-year-old midfielder turned down Wolverhampton Wanderers and an offer to be the player-manager of Cardiff City to instead join Burkinshaw's emerging team.

Yorath was a tough tackler – often booed by opposition fans for his perceived overly aggressive nature. He was exactly the sort of player that Spurs had lacked and would give them the steel they needed to take the next step.

The new campaign began poorly. Despite the addition of Yorath, Tottenham were easily beaten in each of their first three matches. Middlesbrough won 3-1 at White Hart Lane before Norwich smashed Spurs 4-0 and Stoke won 3-1. None of those teams were even contenders, but they had rolled over Spurs. Ricky Villa was dropped after the second defeat, and wouldn't get another chance until mid-September.

Tottenham got their first win of the season against Manchester United in the first leg of the League Cup second round. Spurs' opening goal against United was a sensational volley by Glenn Hoddle after a flicked lay-off from Ossie Ardiles. It was a demonstration of how deadly their midfield could be when they put everything together, but they couldn't put it together again in the second leg as they lost 3-1 to go out 4-3 on aggregate.

One silver lining of the wretched start to the season was the emergence of left-back Chris Hughton. He was a genuine product of the club's youth system, another credit to Pat Welton's work in youth development.

Joining the club as a 13-year-old, Hughton became a full time professional in July 1979 after finishing his apprenticeship as a lift engineer.

Hughton made his debut in the first leg against United and would spend 27 years at the club as a player, coach and twice interim manager, having got his chance because of an injury to Gordon Smith.

Born to a Ghanaian father and Irish mother, Hughton would become an iconic player in a successful Republic of Ireland team and an iconic black footballer.

Between the two legs of the League Cup tie, Spurs got their first league win of the season as Hoddle and Chris Jones scored in a 2-1 win over Manchester City.

The recovery continued with a 2-1 win over Brighton, when Hoddle scored again, and 17-year-old full-back Peter Southey made his sole appearance for the club.[23]

A week later, Spurs were hammered 5-2 at Southampton where, with Burkinshaw still tinkering, young midfielder Stuart Beavon made one of only three first-team appearances.

Spurs were off the bottom but it had been a dreadful start. They were conceding three goals a game. Burkinshaw responded to critics, saying, 'The people who have written us off don't know what they're talking about.'

As in the previous season, Tottenham responded well to adversity and things began to come together after the hammering on the south coast.

They reeled off three 1-1 draws, then won five out of six. The nine-game unbeaten streak lifted them up to fifth, just two points off league leaders Manchester United.

---

23 Southey would sadly die of leukaemia just a few years later.

Paul Miller was suspended, and John Lacy was injured in November, meaning that Tottenham had no recognised senior centre-backs available.

They lost 2-1 to Liverpool at Anfield but even Bill Nicholson's strongest teams had never managed to win that fixture.

But their form again deserted them as the weather turned colder. The Anfield defeat was followed by a point at Goodison Park a week later, and then came four defeats in five matches, culminating with yet another north London derby loss on Boxing Day.

Against Arsenal, goalkeeper Milija Aleksic's error gave Alan Sunderland an easy opener. At the other end Pat Jennings remained impeccable – four years after Spurs had deemed him finished – and he denied Gerry Armstrong and John Pratt equalisers in the first half.

In the second half the match bogged down and finished scrappily, and at the final whistle Tony Galvin and Arsenal's David O'Leary nearly came to blows and had to be separated.

In January, Spurs got a measure of revenge on Manchester United – who had ended their FA Cup campaign the previous season – by beating them in the third round. It took a replay, and Ardiles scored in both matches, but the game became famous for a different reason.

Aleksic was stretchered off with a suspected broken jaw after a collision with Joe Jordan, and Glenn Hoddle took over as goalkeeper in the 57th minute.

Hoddle made one impressive save to deny Steve Coppell, but was well protected by his defenders who held out until the end of 90 minutes and with the sides still deadlocked at 0-0, 30 minutes of extra time were required to split them.

Three minutes from time, Pratt – the substitute who had replaced Aleksic – swung in a high, high cross from the right which eventually fell to Villa on the left of the United box.

The tall, muscular Argentinian held off one defender and looked up for help. Sensing his moment, Ardiles dashed away from his marker. Villa spotted him and made the short pass. Ardiles let the ball run and opened his body up to curl a shot beyond Gary Bailey and into the net.

Ardiles said afterwards, 'This was my most magic moment in England. I was very tired. I had cramp in both my legs and I had to put everything that was left in my strength into it to hit the ball. I was so tired I couldn't even jump for joy after it went in.'

Spurs and United had faced each other nine times in 12 months, and this was just the second victory for Tottenham.

Aleksic lost five teeth in the collision with Jordan, but the Scotland striker visited him in hospital to apologise for what both players considered a freak accident.

On 26 January Spurs managed only a goalless draw away to Swindon in the fourth round, ensuring yet another replay, but Armstrong scored twice to secure progress.

Next came a 3-1 win over Birmingham City. A crowd of just under 50,000 saw Hoddle score twice and Armstrong add another goal and Spurs had reached the last eight for the second straight season, matching their best run in the competition in nearly a decade.

Each of Tottenham's FA Cup ties so far had also been selected for live broadcast on ITV, showing their rising star had caught the eye of television executives.

Spurs drew Liverpool in the quarter-final. Hoddle, a doubt with injury, recovered to start at White Hart Lane. Terry Yorath played with a broken toe. Mark Falco, now 19, was rewarded for goals against Coventry and Leeds with a starting spot alongside Armstrong.

A crowd of 48,000 packed the old ground, and the atmosphere was boisterous despite the players wearing black armbands to mark the death of former Football League secretary Alan Hardaker.

Hoddle started badly and was limping inside the first five minutes, suggesting that he perhaps wasn't fully match fit.

Graeme Souness hurt Villa with a two-footed tackle that would in later years have been a red card. The Argentinian tried to run it off but had to be replaced by Pratt after just 15 minutes.

Spurs were on top but Liverpool looked deadly every time they picked up possession and countered. Their one-touch passing slashed through Tottenham's defence time and again.

The match was finely balanced when Ardiles, playing out virtually from his own corner flag, passed the ball straight to Terry McDermott. McDermott flicked it up and volleyed it beyond Barry Daines to give Liverpool the lead with a magnificent goal in the 37th minute.

When Kenny Dalglish surged into the Spurs box early in the second half, it seemed certain the Scot would make it 2-0 but Daines denied him with some excellent goalkeeping. Minutes later, Liverpool were unfortunate to not be awarded a penalty when Miller floored Dalglish.

Spurs barely got a kick for long stretches of the second half, but while it remained 1-0 there was still hope. Hoddle almost caught out Clemence with a lob late on, winning a corner when the England goalkeeper had to push the shot over the bar.

The home side were building momentum and pouring numbers forward in search of an equaliser but then Liverpool broke. Daines committed and missed, and Dalglish found himself unmarked with an open goal. Somehow the man who would be King Kenny put his shot over the bar.

Still Spurs came forward but wave after wave of their attacks crashed on the rocks of Liverpool's defence.

When the final whistle blew, there was relief on the faces of the Liverpool players and regret for Spurs, as for two years in a row their season essentially ended with an FA Cup quarter-final defeat in March.

Scotland beat Portugal 4-1 in a European Championship qualifier two weeks later. In the crowd was Keith Burkinshaw, there to see Steve Archibald. Archibald didn't start but he came off the bench to score, and Burkinshaw was convinced.

That month he made his first move for the Scot but was initially rebuffed. Aberdeen steadfastly refused to enter negotiations until the Scottish title was won. Crystal Palace were also pushing for Archibald, who was desperate to make a move to England and experience the First Division.

In April, Arsenal had advanced to the semi-final of the UEFA Cup Winners' Cup and asked Spurs to postpone the north London derby in order to prepare. Tottenham declined. Arsenal rotated heavily but still beat Tottenham for the fifth derby in a row. Jones got Spurs' first goal against the Gunners in nearly four years, but it wasn't enough.

With the season winding down, Pratt left to join Portland Timbers in the NASL. Pratt had been at the club for 15 years and played a role in both the highs of the 1960s and the lows of the following decade. He played every game in the promotion-winning season and was virtually ever-present in the following campaign, too. It was rather unfortunate that he was to miss Tottenham's ultimate return to the top.

Tottenham's season had once again promised much but ended with a whimper. They won one, drew two and lost one of their four remaining matches to finish in mid-table again.

The FA Cup run had been solidly impressive, and helped to swell the club's bank accounts. The Liverpool quarter-final alone had generated £100,000 in ticket sales.

32

The icing on the cake

THE 1979/80 season had largely echoed the previous campaign. Spurs had been easily safe, but were far off the title-winning pace of the leading clubs. They had even scored and conceded almost the exact same number of goals (they improved by one in each category).

Crucially, Glenn Hoddle had emerged as a genuine superstar. The 22-year-old playmaker had scored 22 goals in a wildly successful season for him personally, and had even made his England debut, scoring in a win over Bulgaria at Wembley. Keith Burkinshaw needed to build a team worthy of Hoddle and his Argentinian team-mates.

Spurs hadn't had a forward score more than ten goals in the First Division since 1976, and Burkinshaw knew he needed an outlet for the creative brilliance he had in midfield.

In 1979/80, seven different players – Mark Falco, Chris Jones, Gerry Armstrong, Colin Lee, Terry Gibson, John Pratt and Tony Galvin – wore the number nine shirt.

Since the departures of John Duncan and Ian Moores in 1978, Tottenham still hadn't signed a new forward. Terry Yorath had occasionally been deployed in that role during the previous season, alongside Jones and Armstrong, and young Falco played occasionally but wasn't ready to lead the line alone.

Tottenham just didn't have the firepower to match their star-studded midfield, and Burkinshaw knew it.

They had also failed in a bid to sign Cambridge United striker Alan Biley in January. Despite a £300,000 offer, Biley stayed and helped Cambridge win promotion to the Second Division. He eventually made it to the top flight with Derby County.

Having watched Steve Archibald in the flesh, Burkinshaw knew he was exactly what Tottenham were missing and on 11 May 1980 the deal was struck between Spurs and Aberdeen for the 23-year-old striker. He cost £750,000, overtaking Ardiles as the club's record signing.

Aberdeen manager Alex Ferguson described the loss of Archibald as 'the saddest day in my football life'.

Archibald had just helped Ferguson to end the Old Firm's 15-year hold on the Scottish title, and had even rejected a significant pay raise from Aberdeen in order to see the move through. Ferguson predicted that he would 'do a great job for Tottenham' after the months-long negotiations were finally completed.

At the time, the world transfer record was still Paolo Rossi, signed from Vicenza by Juventus for £1.75m in 1976. Andy Gray's £1.469m move from Aston Villa to Wolves in 1979 remained the British peak.

That same month saw Tottenham sign Graham Roberts. Spurs' discovery of Roberts featured a series of remarkable coincidences. Bill Nicholson had been scheduled to drive to a match but had felt ill, so he decided to instead attend a fixture to which he could take a train.

Awaiting his return train after the match, during which the player he had gone to see had been unimpressive, Nicholson began speaking with a man who had also been present. The individual turned out to be a great fan of non-league football and told Nicholson that the best non-league team in the country was Weymouth. He went on to say they had two great players, Graham Roberts and another whose name he couldn't remember.

Nicholson only needed to see Roberts play once – a match in which he scored twice and ran the game from midfield – before recommending him to Burkinshaw.

Spurs agreed to pay £20,000 and to play a friendly against Weymouth in exchange for the young midfielder.

Burkinshaw didn't even know what kind of player he was buying. His first question upon meeting Roberts was, 'What position do you play?' But Nicholson's recommendation was enough.

The first meeting went well and Roberts was convinced that Spurs was the best option for him, despite West Bromwich Albion also trying to sign him.

Roberts was on such a small wage – less than £200 per week – that new team-mate Gerry Armstrong had to help him carpet his house by convincing a contractor friend to delay requesting payment of his bill.

The new signing made his first appearance in an end of season friendly against a combined Rapid Vienna and FC Austria XI.

Not happy with just adding Archibald, Burkinshaw moved for England under-21 striker Garth Crooks in July.

According to legend, Crooks had been scouted by Stoke City's then manager Tony Waddington as a boy, kicking a ball against the wall of the Potters' Victoria Ground. Breaking out at the age of 18, and eventually scoring over 50 goals for Stoke, Crooks had helped them achieve promotion back to the First Division in 1979. He was their top scorer in the next campaign with 15 goals as they barely avoided relegation, an experience Crooks described as 'traumatic', adding, 'I feel as though a move would do me good.'

After that declaration, Birmingham City, Crystal Palace and Spurs expressed their interest in signing him. Crooks had played alongside former Spurs winger Jimmy Robertson at Stoke and that may have helped sway him towards picking a move to White Hart Lane.

Stoke were reluctant to sell a promising young striker, but needed the cash to finance a deal for St Mirren defender Iain Munro and Shrewsbury Town forward Paul Maguire.

At the end of July, Crooks travelled to White Hart Lane to meet with Burkinshaw. The following day the £600,000 transfer was announced.

Crooks was excited at the prospect of playing alongside 'world-class players'. He found a close friend and kindred spirit in Ossie Ardiles, in whose generosity he saw a reflection of his own values.

While playing at Tottenham, Crooks studied political science at North London University. Passionate about the rights of his fellow professionals, he eventually rose to chair the PFA.

Crooks would become both a great goalscorer, and a scorer of important goals. When Tottenham broke a 73-year winless streak at Anfield in 1985, Crooks scored the winner. When Spurs ended a 14-year run without lifting the FA Cup in 1981, again it was Crooks who scored a crucial goal. His goal in that final would make him the first Black player to score in an FA Cup Final.

One – or both – of Archibald and Crooks would be Spurs' top scorer for each of the next four seasons, and Burkinshaw described the duo as 'the icing on the cake', but first the duo would need to develop chemistry.

Crooks already knew Hoddle from the England under-21 team. They had played together three times in February, March and April of 1980.

Spurs had lacked attacking quality, but in particular pace. Both Crooks and Archibald provided real speed. Crooks especially lived to attack the space behind a high line.

Archibald scored on his pre-season debut as Spurs drew with Southend, and Crooks made his first appearance in pre-season against Portsmouth, when Falco scored the winner. Spurs were beaten 4-2 by PSV next, before Crooks and Archibald finally got their first game together. The new strikers started as a pair in a pre-season match against Rangers at Ibrox but neither scored. Crooks got his first goal in a 4-1 defeat against Dundee United.

Spurs lost their final preparation match, 1-0 against Swansea City. While pre-season ultimately counts for nothing, it did not augur well that their expensively assembled team had lost four out of six matches, most of which had been against lesser opposition.

Crooks would eventually reflect that he struggled in that pre-season. For him and Archibald, it seemed as if the team was run by and for the midfield.

Crooks explained later that while he didn't see Burkinshaw as a particularly adept tactician, the coach knew how to put a team together, 'He could see a player's talent quickly and crucially could see how to assemble the jigsaw.'

Burkinshaw had now put together a team that was capable of challenging for honours, but first they had to learn to play like one.

With Hoddle, Ardiles and Ricardo Villa as the core of the side, the attackers felt starved of possession. They would develop an excellent partnership, partly in a direct response to the midfield's reluctance to pass them the ball.

Hoddle and Ardiles particularly would pass to the forwards and expect an immediate return ball, so after one especially frustrating training session Crooks and Archibald decided to try to keep the ball.

The emergence of the new strike partnership was hugely significant for Hoddle, too. In his autobiography, the Spurs legend explained, 'It was a breakthrough moment for me because I finally had two strikers whose pace and movement allowed me to drop dangerous balls behind unsuspecting defenders. That was my real art: always looking to play forward and be creative in possession. Previous team-mates weren't quite on my wavelength, or they didn't have the pace or movement to make my through balls come off. But these two had pace and they knew where to run. Crooksy was electrifying and Archie had an eerie ability to sniff out a goal.'

In the summer of 1980, Ardiles cut short his summer holidays to take part in the filming of *Escape to Victory*. The movie, based (very roughly) on a true story, starred Sylvester Stallone, Michael Caine, and Pelé.

Ardiles spent the month of June in Hungary, staying up late every night swapping stories with the actors. England legend Bobby Moore was also involved, and so too were various Ipswich players.

The story featured a team of concentration camp prisoners playing against a German team. It was set in Paris, but filmed in a real former concentration camp in Hungary. Ardiles was moved by his experience. The conditions shocked him. He would always remember that even in June it was bitterly cold in the barracks.

The film was directed by Hollywood legend John Huston, director of *The Treasure of the Sierra Madre* – for which he won the Oscar for Best Director – *The Maltese Falcon*, *The Red Badge of Courage* and *The African Queen*.

Ardiles was supposed to be playing a speaking role, but he demurred once on set. He feared his English skills, as much as his acting talent, were not good enough. As a result, his character, Carlos Rey, became a silent part.

Ardiles says much of the football footage in the movie is not choreographed – as had been the plan – but instead was just edited footage of the pros messing about on the pitch. Ardiles's character scores a goal in the film. According to him, 'It followed one of the best bits of playmaking I think I've ever done in my life.'

Afterwards, Huston turned to him and said, 'Ossie, the camera didn't get it all so can you do it again please?'

The film culminates with Stallone's character saving a penalty, which Ardiles says took over 30 attempts. England

World Cup winner Gordon Banks was recruited to help improve the Oscar-winner's goalkeeping for the film.

Tottenham made two major decisions in the summer of 1980, away from the playing staff. The first was the appointment of Peter Shreeves as assistant manager, although, technically it was Peter Shreeve who got the new job. He would become known as Shreeves, but his family name was actually Shreeve. The Welshman simply gave up on correcting people, and became Shreeves.

It was his third promotion since joining the club in 1974 under Terry Neill. First he had been appointed as youth coach, where he had helped bring through the likes of Hoddle and Paul Miller, before moving up to reserve team manager after Spurs were relegated. Burkinshaw, appreciating Shreeves's influence, brought him directly into his coaching staff for the 1980/81 season.

Shreeves would eventually succeed Burkinshaw in the top job at Tottenham, and return for a second spell in charge in the early 1990s.

The other change that summer was somewhat less positive. The looming old West Stand, the same one that Ardiles and Villa had posed in front of when first signing for Tottenham, was demolished. The work began in November, reducing capacity at White Hart Lane right at the moment when anticipation was really blossoming among the supporters. There was a notion that Burkinshaw was finally going to deliver on three years of promise and tickets became extremely hard to come by.

Fans standing on the Shelf could soon see London buses rolling down Tottenham High Road in the middle of matches as the old stand came down. The construction would overrun both budget and schedule, which had a doubly negative impact on Spurs' balance sheets. Not only did they have to pay more than anticipated, their incomes were reduced by White Hart Lane's shrunken capacity.

With that cut in attendances, ticket prices rose in 1980 and Spurs soon had one of the more expensive season tickets in British football. Fans had to pay £62, which was admittedly far cheaper than Arsenal's league-leading £84.

By the time the new stand was inaugurated in 1982, Tottenham were in over £4m of debt. Chairman Sidney Wale would soon be compelled to sell his controlling interest in the club to property developer Irving Scholar, with long-lasting consequences.

33

The comeback starts here

SPURS WERE given 25/1 odds to win the First Division in 1980/81. Liverpool were favourites, with Manchester United, Nottingham Forest, Ipswich and Arsenal all on shorter odds. However, the *Liverpool Echo* predicted Tottenham as the only team that could upset Liverpool's likely championship win.

Tottenham opened the new season against Brian Clough's Forest, the two-time reigning European champions, who had finished fifth the year before.

Ossie Ardiles's clever twisting in the box won a penalty which Glenn Hoddle converted before half-time to open the scoring. Hoddle was again at the heart of things after the break, setting up Garth Crooks for a debut goal. Crooks took the pass and sidestepped England goalkeeper Peter Shilton – a former team-mate at Stoke City – before finishing into an empty net.

Tottenham won 2-0 and the new strike partnership had made an instant impact. Steve Archibald's physical strength and bravery seemed the perfect complement to Crooks's skills and pace. Archibald said after the match, 'It was the sort of home debut you pray for.'

The excitement among the fans spread to the players after the final whistle, and Keith Burkinshaw felt compelled to calm them down. He told his squad, 'We mustn't go overboard about one performance. We had some fine wins last season, but lacked consistency. We'll see against Palace.'

Clive Allen – the son of Tottenham's Double-winning forward Les – had joined Crystal Palace that summer from Arsenal, with full-back Kenny Sansom going the other way.

Arsenal themselves had signed Allen from QPR for a First Division record fee of £1.25m in the same window.

Allen wrote in his autobiography that Spurs had also been interested in buying him, but delayed their move and missed out. He would eventually join Tottenham in 1984 and set a record for their most goals in a single season in 1987 with 49.

But that was all in the future. For now, Allen had been sold without playing a competitive fixture for the Gunners, although he had made several appearances in a disastrous pre-season. So poor a fit had Allen proven to be that before the opening match of the season, Terry Neill told him he was 'surplus to requirements' and informed him that he could speak to Crystal Palace.

Palace manager Terry Venables was widely thought to be building a special team. The press had crowned them 'the team of the '80s' in anticipation of their young stars fulfilling their promise in the coming years.

Importantly for Allen, Venables promised to play him as a centre-forward, not out on the wing as Neill had done at Arsenal.

The full explanation of this bizarre double transfer has never been given, although conspiracy theories abound. One idea floated was that QPR had refused to sell Allen to Palace directly because of their owners' personal enmity towards Venables and so Arsenal had agreed to act as intermediary.

Another notion presented at the time was that Palace wanted Allen but had no cash to buy him, so swapping Sansom was the only way they could get him.

Neither of these ideas make a great deal of sense, given that Allen played in pre-season matches in which he could have been injured, ending any hopes of completing the convoluted deal.

Crooks said before the Palace match, 'It has never been more important to go out and entertain, and that's something Tottenham have always believed in. That's the main reason I came here. Palace play the same way, so it should be quite a game.'

With the anticipation as high as could be, the authorities set a crowd limit of 38,000 at Selhurst Park.

Crooks headed in a Hoddle corner, before racing past lunging defenders to put Spurs 2-0 up inside 17 minutes. Palace midfielder Vince Hilaire then pulled one back for the home side.

Just before half-time Hoddle restored Spurs' two-goal lead with a tremendous volley, the sort that was quickly becoming something of a trademark.

Palace scored again to make it 3-2 after an error from Chris Hughton shortly after the hour mark, and minutes later Hilaire was sent off for pushing the referee to the ground – earning a four-match ban as a result – after being unhappy at being denied a foul following a Crooks tackle.

Archibald then scored his first Tottenham goal, before Palace scored yet again, leaving the match dramatically poised at 4-3 with ten minutes left, but

Spurs held on to make it two wins from two.

Crooks had wanted entertainment, and both sides had certainly provided it, but Tottenham had shown a concerning defensive shakiness.

After the win, Crooks and Archibald were labelled an 'overnight success' as a partnership. Archibald explained, 'It's not just luck that Garth and I have hit it off. We have worked very hard in training and will continue to do so.'

By contrast to Spurs' firing forwards, Allen had now gone five games without a goal but he scored a hat-trick in Palace's next match as they beat Middlesbrough 5-2.

Next up for Spurs was Brighton & Hove Albion. Another win would make it their best start to a season in 20 years.

Seagulls manager Alan Mullery was welcomed back to White Hart Lane with a standing ovation, but his team were not there to just make up the numbers.

Brighton midfielder Ray McHale was hit on the head by a coin, thrown by a Tottenham fan, as he went to take a throw-in. He avoided any serious injury and joked after the match that his main annoyance was that he never found the coin. The referee, a horde of policemen and even Mullery charged towards the spot in the crowd from which the coin had come, but the match was quickly resumed.

A lovely reverse pass from Hoddle set Villa away before the Argentinian fired in his cross and Crooks slid in to convert in the 34th minute.

Brighton equalised just before half-time when an awkward bounce caused Mark Kendall to freeze in the Spurs goal.

Hoddle put Tottenham ahead again after the break – in truth Brighton keeper Graham Moseley deserved more credit, having effectively thrown the ball into his own net – but the visitors levelled with 12 minutes to play.

In the first half Spurs had looked like winning easily, but by the end they were lucky to hold on for a draw, although despite that disappointment they were level at the top with Ipswich Town, Aston Villa and Southampton.

After a League Cup second round first leg win over Leyton Orient, Tottenham faced a real test in the form of Terry Neill's Arsenal.

Burkinshaw had still never beaten Arsenal as a manager and Terry Yorath said before the match, 'We really want to win this one. For Keith more than anyone else.'

The *Daily Mirror* warned that Spurs' commitment to attack would leave them open to the 'famous Arsenal sucker punch'.

Crooks was dealing with a groin injury, but started nonetheless, and Spurs dominated the first half but Pat Jennings's typical brilliance kept them at bay. Twice Crooks was denied by excellent saves, and he put a third shot just wide of the post. Right before half-time Jennings could only push Villa's shot into the path of Archibald, but the Scot put his shot over the bar.

Tottenham's own defence looked fragile once again. Arsenal midfielder Graham Rix proved the difference, playing two defence-splitting passes to David Price and Frank Stapleton in the second half. Goalkeeper Kendall was blamed for both goals.

Peter Taylor, on as a late substitute, did beat Jennings late, but John Devine cleared his shot off the line, and despite the optimism coming into the match, Spurs once again fell to defeat in the north London derby without even scoring a goal.

Leyton Orient were finished off in the League Cup in midweek as Crooks and Archibald both scored again, and Tottenham's strike partners earned a new nickname, 'the Terrible Twins'. It was a spiteful clash, with Crooks scuffling with Orient captain Tommy Taylor in the tunnel after the final whistle. Worse, Yorath was reported to the FA for allegedly dropping his shorts 'as tempers flared'.

'There is a mood of confidence running through the side,' Burkinshaw told reporters before the visit of Manchester United in the next First Division fixture.

Tottenham dominated for 75 minutes, but failed to convert that strong position into goals as Villa, Hughton, and Hoddle tested Gary Bailey but couldn't find the breakthrough.

Burkinshaw then took Ardiles off for Taylor and saw his team fall to pieces. United, having looked lost, suddenly took control and were unlucky not to find a winner.

Burkinshaw admitted afterwards that the substitution had been a gamble, saying, 'If we'd scored, I'd be a great fellow. We didn't – I'm considered stupid.'

Ardiles didn't mind being taken off. Spurs had played seven matches in 22 days to begin their season, and the players were exhausted. Ardiles gave an interview after the draw against United, saying as much. He told the *Daily Mirror* that Spurs' packed schedule had 'hit me very hard this year, and I'm feeling extremely tired'. The Argentinian, who was close to signing a new contract, explained that his team-mates were faring no better, 'I spoke to Ricky and Glen about my problem. They both admitted they feel exactly the same. They would have been happy to be replaced.'

Hoddle was playing on an achilles injury, something which was aggravated during the United match, and as a result the star midfielder was forced to drop out of the England squad for a World Cup qualifier against Norway.

Next for Spurs was a trip to Elland Road to face Leeds, who by this stage were a fading force. The mighty team of the early 1970s was long gone. In fact, they would be relegated the following season and spend a decade in the Second Division.

They had started the season disastrously, losing four of their first five matches to sit bottom of the table. Their manager Jimmy Adamson had resigned in midweek following a fan revolt. Since Don Revie's departure in 1974, Brian Clough, Jimmy Armfield, Jock Stein and Adamson had come and gone in the Elland Road hotseat.

As so often happens, Leeds looked vastly improved in the first match after their manager's departure.

Spurs dominated, with Taylor hitting the post and crossbar, but in the absence of Terry Yorath they struggled to win the battle in midfield. The Welshman was absent as he struggled to resolve a hamstring issue.

Archibald was at the centre of the action, twice going close but also playing as the focal point of Tottenham's attacks.

Villa was named man of the match, with Archibald not far behind, but Leeds gave their best performance of the season. 'I wouldn't think Leeds had fought as hard as that all season,' Burkinshaw said, having watched his team drop another point with their second straight goalless draw.

Arsenal, Manchester United, and now Leeds – Tottenham had gone nearly 300 minutes of league football without scoring a goal. The brilliant performances of the opening weeks of the season seemed a long way off.

Promoted Sunderland, who had made a strong start to the season, were Spurs' next opponents, but instead of rediscovering their scoring touch Tottenham slid further with their third straight goalless draw.

Taylor was good again, setting up Crooks, Archibald and Villa with scoring chances. Crooks almost produced a goal with a brilliant piece of skill, somehow squeezing between two defenders before shooting wide.

The matches against Manchester United and Leeds had been relatively strong performances with Spurs a touch unfortunate in each. Against Sunderland, there was no such optimistic view.

Spurs were perfectly capable of reaching the opposition box but seemed incapable of going any further. They were described as 'inept', the Crooks and Archibald partnership which had seemed so promising had seemingly dissolved, and Hoddle – once considered the future of England's midfield – was the subject of more than one scathing column. *The People* christened Tottenham's ongoing struggles in front of goal 'the nil-nil desperandum show'.

Yorath returned for Spurs' next match – a League Cup tie against Crystal Palace – but the goals did not come with him. Palace, bottom of the league with one win and six defeats after conceding 21 goals, managed to eke out a 0-0 draw.

Goalkeeper Paul Barron, who had played every minute for Palace so far, was dropped in advance only to find himself back in the starting line-up when his replacement, John Burridge, refused to play due to a contract dispute.

Barron shone, keeping out long-range strikes from Yorath and Villa. Villa was booked when he raced in to defend Ardiles from the wrath of Gerry Francis in a minor scuffle.

Remarkably, Tottenham had failed to score a goal in four straight matches, and five of their last six. Only Leyton Orient, against whom Spurs had scored three, had failed to keep their misfiring attack at bay.

Burkinshaw praised the dropped but reinstated goalkeeper, saying, 'The only difference between us and not scoring was Paul Barron.'

Villa broke Tottenham's 448-minute goal drought when he scored the opener against Leicester City, but unfortunately Leicester scored twice in reply to beat Spurs 2-1 and leave them marooned in mid-table. It was not a vintage Leicester side. The Foxes had scored just four goals and the victory was only their third of the season.

Just three days after that defeat, Tottenham faced Crystal Palace in a League Cup third round replay. Another trip to Selhurst Park, for Spurs' fourth game in ten days, did not seem like the solution to their woes.

Burkinshaw, incensed at the cynicism Leicester had displayed in their victory against Tottenham, said, 'There is no doubt that Saturday's result was a travesty of justice and it certainly won't change our policy. I believe that with gates dwindling, teams must set out to entertain the paying customers, so we shall continue to go forward.'

His footballing idealism would not be compromised, even with a tie against Arsenal – awaiting in the next round of the cup – on the line. 'You don't need much more incentive to win,' Burkinshaw added.

Graham Roberts had been plugging away in reserve matches, still yet to make his debut, but was included as the substitute against Palace.

Just after the hour, Hoddle and Palace's Jerry Murphy were sent off for violent conduct with the match level at 1-1. Clive Allen had scored against his future team, while Hoddle had equalised with a magnificent 20-yard free kick in front of watching England manager Ron Greenwood.

No one, including Burkinshaw, saw the red card incident but both sides had been reduced to ten men. Terry Venables said afterwards that Murphy's version of the story was that he had pulled Hoddle's shirt, and the England midfielder had elbowed him in retaliation.

Crooks missed a penalty with four minutes to play and the match went to extra time. There, Villa – who had conceded the penalty for Palace's opener – set up Crooks to put Spurs ahead, before sealing victory with a goal of his own. Tottenham had finally managed to both score and win.

It had been a rough tie. In addition to Hoddle and Murphy's dismissals, seven other players had been booked across the two matches.

But Spurs still hadn't won a league game since August, although that changed a few days later on a trip to Stoke when they won by the odd goal in five.

Taylor scored an early penalty, won by former Stoke forward Crooks. Villa ghosted through the Stoke defence to set up Archibald for another goal, and Chris Hughton added a third.

A week later Spurs won another 3-2 thriller, this time against Middlesbrough. Steve Perryman, furious that the linesman had failed to flag Boro's late equaliser for offside, charged forward to set up Archibald's winner.

The captain was more relieved than anything as his team had won a home league match for the first time since the opening day of the season. He said, 'We've disappointed the fans a few times at home. So when that goal [Boro's equaliser] stood, I told the lads to keep it tight and not get mugged again. Next thing I'm up in their box setting up the winner.'

Ardiles was forced off with an injury and missed the next match, a trip to Aston Villa, where Spurs were roughed up in losing 3-0. They lost again a few days later against Manchester City.

Burkinshaw had rotated his exhausted side, with Taylor and Gerry Armstrong making rare starts. It was the final Tottenham appearance for each of them; Armstrong would join Watford, while Taylor would move to Orient.

The City match had been rescheduled from earlier in the season and forced Spurs' League Cup clash with Arsenal to be moved. It was probably for the best, as Spurs' form had deserted them again.

Ardiles returned and brought Tottenham's form with him as they thrashed Coventry City 4-1. Archibald, who had scored twice against Coventry, then made it four goals in two games with another brace against Everton in a 2-2 draw.

34

The Spurs go marching

SPURS HAD worked their way into mid-table after their poor start, and focus now switched to the League Cup clash against Arsenal on 4 November 1980.

The Gunners were on the longest winning streak in the history of the north London derby. They travelled to Tottenham on a freezing night after six straight victories and defending an eight-match unbeaten run.

Pat Jennings wasn't in the Arsenal team, but Willie Young was, and Ricky Villa had the ball in the net early only for his goal to be ruled out by the referee.

Twenty-four minutes into a frantic clash, Villa played in Garth Crooks. Crooks looked up and flashed in a cross which was deflected off Young and directly into the path of Ossie Ardiles who swooped to put Tottenham ahead.

Daines had to make at least two brilliant saves – he was even credited by Gunners manager Terry Neill for an impressive display – but Arsenal were unable to sustain pressure and Tottenham could have doubled their lead late when Villa went through but saw his shot saved.

Keith Burkinshaw was delighted with a long-awaited victory, saying, 'This is the best result we've had since I became manager. It's always nice to win but to beat that lot is icing on the cake.'

Tottenham had finally beaten their old manager, and at full time the crowd sang 'Glory, Glory, Hallelujah', something they had notably not done for some time. Over 42,000 people were present but, with demolition work beginning on the West Stand, it would be 18 months before a similar crowd would again be able to fit into White Hart Lane.

Crooks and Archibald then combined for six goals in the next three matches, all victories, as Spurs climbed to ninth.

On 17 November Tottenham hammered Weymouth 6-1 in a friendly. Ardiles and Villa both scored braces, but it would be the last time they would taste victory for a month.

They lost their next four games, each by a single goal. West Ham knocked them out of the League Cup before they were also beaten at Liverpool, as was virtually a tradition.

Ardiles missed most of this run having been given permission to leave the team and join up with Argentina for the world champions' Gold Cup in Uruguay. The tournament was a celebration of the 50th anniversary of the first World Cup. The six former winners were invited, but England declined to participate.

For the first time, Ardiles was playing alongside Diego Maradona. The future legend would become close with the Spurs midfielder, eventually playing in his testimonial. That match, at White Hart Lane in 1986, created the famous image of Maradona in a Tottenham shirt.

The mini tournament ended with Uruguay beating Brazil 2-1 in the final. Argentina had not lost either of their two matches, but finished second in their group.

Wins over Manchester City and Ipswich steadied Spurs' ship before a bad 4-1 defeat to Middlesbrough. Consecutive draws then rounded out the year, and Tottenham entered 1981 sitting tenth. In a crowded league table, they were only four points off fourth-placed Arsenal.

The new year began with the hope that, in a year ending in one, Tottenham could finally break their trophy drought. The tradition of Tottenham winning trophies in years ending in one is little more than a statistical quirk but it is certainly interesting that by 1981, Spurs had already collected silverware in 1901, 1921, 1951, 1961, and 1971.

Having already exited the League Cup and being well off the pace of First Division leaders Aston Villa, that hope was consigned to the FA Cup.

Tottenham's first opponents were Queens Park Rangers in the third round. Ardiles was still unavailable but Burkinshaw otherwise picked a strong team. Crooks, Archibald, Hoddle, Villa, Steve Perryman and Terry Yorath all started.

QPR were a mid-table Second Division team at the time, but they earned a goalless draw and forced a replay, although back at White Hart Lane, Spurs were all business.

Garry Brooke, who had made his debut at the end of November, floated a cross to the far post for Crooks to open the scoring, and Spurs capped a dominant first half with a delightful team goal. Hoddle picked up possession in his own half and lofted a pass for Tony Galvin, who played a one-two with Crooks on the edge of the area before lobbing the goalkeeper.

QPR pulled one back but Tottenham sealed victory with their third. Archibald displayed great strength and no lack of skill to hold off two defenders and play in Hoddle, who scored the decisive goal.

Ten days later, Spurs faced Arsenal again. They got off to the perfect start when Hoddle chipped a ball into Archibald at the top of the box. The Scottish number nine controlled the pass with his chest before hitting a low volley beyond Jennings. It was the first time Jennings had conceded against Spurs.

The pair almost repeated the trick minutes later when Hoddle floated in a free kick towards the far post. Catching Jennings flat-footed, Archibald slid in but the veteran goalkeeper managed to grab the goalbound shot.

Next, Paul Miller headed a Hoddle free kick down to Archibald but his shot was wild and flew over the bar.

Early in the second half Arsenal had their best spell and Barry Daines was repeatedly called into action. He was paid the ultimate compliment by the television coverage which suggested his saves were worthy of 'the man at the other end'.

Archibald thought he'd sealed victory when he ran on to a Hoddle pass and fired past Jennings into the net, but he was flagged offside.

After an excellent display, when Archibald's second goal did come it was one of the scrappiest of his career. In the 89th minute Arsenal midfielder John Devine attempted a clearance in his own box, but badly mis-kicked the ball and it fell straight to Archibald, who rather scuffed his shot into the net.

This time the fans didn't even wait until the final whistle to begin singing 'Glory, Glory, Hallelujah' as they celebrated their first league win over the old enemy since April 1976.

A week after the derby victory, Ardiles returned to the line-up for the FA Cup fourth round tie against Hull City. Tottenham were dominating but shortly after Crooks had a header miraculously saved, Hull almost took a shock lead. Daines, who had just been awarded a testimonial, raced off his line to try to cut out a long ball from the visitors, but was caught in no man's land and could only watch Keith Edwards's lob fly over his head towards goal. Thankfully, it bounced about a foot wide of Daines's left-hand upright.

Tottenham continued to dominate after the break but couldn't find a breakthrough and a replay beckoned. Seven minutes from time though, Brooke – on as a substitute for Ardiles – tried a pot shot from distance which dipped and beat the Hull keeper.

Five minutes later Crooks slipped a pass to Archibald in the box, the Scot spinning and making it 2-0 with his left foot.

Spurs had been considered likely candidates to win the FA Cup from the start of the season, but their hopes had only grown with some solid victories. The fact that league leaders Aston Villa, Arsenal and Liverpool had already been knocked out didn't hurt either.

In February, the new Thatcher government abandoned plans to close 23 mines following protest from the National Union of Mineworkers. The union had threatened strikes, and with the memory of 1972 and 1974 fresh in the minds of a weary public, the government conceded; 240,000 miners had been ready to launch an indefinite strike which would have once again paralysed a country still dependent on coal.

Twenty-one fans were killed and 55 were injured in the Karaiskakis Stadium disaster in Piraeus, Greece, following a match between Olympiacos and AEK Athens. The incident apparently occurred as fans tried to leave the stadium, but were unable to get through the wrongfully closed gate.

Immigration outpaced emigration in Britain in 1981 for the first time in decades, something that has remained true almost consistently ever since. The changing face of Britain and the emergence of a cosmopolitan, modern nation was something reflected in Tottenham's relatively diverse team.

The modern English Premier League is far more diverse still, but Spurs' handful of non-British players helped to build the foundations upon which it was built.

That month too, the Chinese New Year saw the end of the year of the monkey and the beginning of the year of the rooster.

Valentine's Day in 1981 saw the next step in Spurs' FA Cup journey: a date with Coventry City. Hughton was back in the line-up after six weeks out with injury, while Hoddle passed a late fitness test to also start.

With the West Stand now fully demolished, the sun was streaming down on White Hart Lane as Graham Roberts unleashed a powerful early shot that just flew over the crossbar. Ardiles was then the next to go close, flashing a volley just wide.

Fifteen minutes in Ardiles made a run but the pass never came. As a consequence, the Argentinian was lurking behind the Coventry line, in the perfect place to intercept Paul Dyson's back-pass. He rounded the keeper and finished into an empty net to give Tottenham the perfect start.

Archibald made it 2-0 when he beat the Coventry defenders in a race for John Lacy's lob in the 32nd minute, and Crooks was inches from a third when he followed up his own shot, pushing the rebound just wide.

A quick Coventry free kick caught Spurs out and Tommy English made it 2-1, then shortly before half-time Daines was lobbed again but again the attempt missed the open goal.

Coventry added another forward at half-time, bringing on Mark Hateley who should have equalised with his first touch, a header over the bar, as both sides were going for it and the opportunities were flowing freely.

Hoddle, sensing his chance, drifted away from his marker and called for the ball. Taking possession on the half turn he fizzed a pass into the feet of Hughton who controlled with one touch and finished with the next to seal victory with ten minutes to play.

It had been Tottenham's 21st time in the fifth round since the end of the Second World War, a record for any club, but the fans were thinking of something more. This time they were singing about Wembley.

A week later, Tottenham suffered their first loss in two months as Leicester won 2-1 at White Hart Lane, but by now their focus was entirely on the cup.

They had reached the quarter-final, what Steve Perryman considered 'the bogey round' after drawing Liverpool and Manchester United in the last two seasons. He believed that they were due some luck in the draw, and they got it when Third Division Exeter City came out of the hat.

The Grecians' fans had brought a cockerel – Tottenham's emblem – and were planning to roast it after the match, but it escaped and caused a delay as stewards chased it around the pitch.

Early in the match Archibald slipped a pass to Crooks, who eliminated his man with a perfect touch and whipped the ball into the net but the linesman flagged and the goal was disallowed.

Minutes later, Archibald was waiting at the far post for Hoddle's chip to drop but an Exeter defender just managed to get a head on the ball and deflect it out for a corner.

When Hoddle did find Archibald soon afterwards, the Scot played a pass across the face of goal towards his strike partner but Crooks's shot went just wide, and the tie was goalless at the break.

After the break, Crooks had another chance but headed over from close range. Tottenham finally got the breakthrough when Hoddle received a short corner and floated a right-footed cross towards the far post for Roberts to head in a rare goal.

In the 73rd minute, Ardiles earned a free kick when he was clattered near the edge of the box. Hoddle hammered it directly at Exeter keeper Len Bond, who stopped the shot, but it scrambled under his legs and Miller reacted fastest to put the loose ball away from close range.

It had been far from their best performance, but – after losing narrowly to Manchester United and Liverpool – Burkinshaw's Spurs had finally passed the quarter-final hurdle.

In the hat with them were Wolverhampton Wanderers, Manchester City and Ipswich Town. Ipswich were the strongest team left in the competition and were widely viewed as the favourites.

35

Wolves, again

SPURS HAD won their second FA Cup against Wolverhampton Wanderers in 1921, while their glorious 1960s team had arguably arrived on the scene with their 5-1 victory over Stan Cullis's Wolves – arguably the great team of the 1950s – in September 1958.

The first UEFA Cup was won over two legs against the same side in 1972. In the same season it was Wolves again standing in Spurs' way in the League Cup semi-final, which was won in extra time before going on to lift the cup at Wembley.

Now, with Tottenham's ascendent team looking to end an eight-year trophy drought and a 14-year stretch without an FA Cup, Wolves were once again cast in the role of opposition in the 1981 semi-final at Hillsborough.

Keith Burkinshaw gambled on the fitness of Ricky Villa – who had played just 45 minutes of football since February – and stuck with Milija Aleksic in goal despite the availability of Barry Daines.

Thinking he was doing them a favour, Burkinshaw told the players the starting line-up the night before but Graham Roberts remembers that they were still nearly overcome with nerves as a result.

At dawn, Roberts, Glenn Hoddle, John Lacy and Aleksic all abandoned efforts to sleep and walked together in the street outside the hotel.

Some 50,174 tickets were sold and Spurs fans stood in the Leppings Lane End which would become infamous eight years later after the Hillsborough disaster, which claimed the lives of 97 Liverpool supporters.

Before kick-off, many of the same details which would become internationally known in 1989 were repeated. Congestion at the turnstiles resulted in the decision to simply open the gates. This meant that the central section of the Leppings Lane end was over capacity by 335.

Despite the Spurs end being full, police and stadium authorities continued to direct more fans in. More than 200 people were unable to get beyond the turnstiles, such was the overcrowding.

Just four minutes into the match, Tony Galvin got a touch on a loose ball at the Wolves end and knocked it beyond the advancing defence. Racing after it and into the box, Galvin played a lovely pass across the face of goal for Steve Archibald to open the scoring with his 25th goal of the season.

Many fans remember a crushing press after Archibald's goal. Rolling waves of humanity surged forward and there were endless shouts to 'stop pushing'. The crush went on and panicking fans began to scale the fences and spill on to the running track behind the goal in an attempt to escape.

Less than a minute later, Kenny Hibbitt got Wolves back level with a low half volley beyond Aleksic.

Even as the match continued, fans who had escaped the crush were sitting on the track, with no sign of authorities taking action. Thirty-eight people were treated for injuries including broken arms, a broken leg and deep gashes. Of these, eight required hospitalisation and match footage captures at least one being carried away on a stretcher.

Speaking afterwards, one supporter described his experience, 'Women and children were being crushed ... I felt my ribs cracking ... The police became aware of the dangerous situation and began letting people on to the touchline.'

The subsequent inquiry heard that the only thing that had avoided deaths was the quick-thinking of an off-duty policeman who ordered the emergency gates opened.

As many as 500 fans ended up on the track, filling much of the space behind the goal. They refused police requests to move to the Wolves end and hundreds watched the remainder of the match from pitchside.

Despite what was essentially a dress rehearsal for tragedy, the authorities failed to take the action which could have reduced or even prevented the disaster which would come eight years later. For those who attended the match, there is an enduring sense that something similar could so easily have happened to them.

It is important to note that the experience of Tottenham fans against Wolves in 1981 was far from the only such incident other than the disaster in 1989. Research reveals[24] major crushes occurred at Hillsborough in 1970, 1957, 1956, 1952, 1934 and 1912. In 1934, a supporter was crushed to death.

Just before half-time in 1981, Hoddle put Spurs back in front with a magnificent free kick which Wolves keeper Paul Bradshaw never even bothered trying to save.

Tottenham seemed to have done enough, and many likely thought they were on their way to Wembley, but in the dying seconds Hibbitt chased a loose ball into the Tottenham box and Hoddle made a desperate tackle. Tottenham's number ten appeared to have taken the ball off Hibbitt's toes, but was harshly judged to have committed a foul.

Archibald was booked, so vehemently did he protest the referee's decision, then Willie Carr converted the ensuing spot-kick and the Spurs players' fury went on.

Burkinshaw ran on to the pitch to calm his players down as they continued to shout at the referee and his assistants.

---

24 Further details at https://tinyurl.com/HillsboroughCrushes

Thirty minutes of extra time was played but the two sides remained level at 2-2, meaning a replay was required.

Perhaps concerned they would talk themselves into trouble, Burkinshaw banned his players from speaking to the media after the match but described the decision as 'a little bit of a shattering experience'.

The Tottenham boss made his opinion clear when he suggested that Hibbitt should be 'in the Olympics, in the swimming'.

Hibbitt himself was free to speak to the press, and admitted that in his opinion, Hoddle had taken the ball cleanly and the referee had been unsighted and forced to guess.

Manchester City won the other semi-final, beating Ipswich Town 1–0 after extra time at Villa Park to earn their place at Wembley.

The replay was set for Highbury – the 12th time that season that Spurs would play a cup tie in London – four days later.

With Tottenham the nominal home side, they occupied the area usually considered 'enemy territory' – the North Bank, the heart of darkness.

Burkinshaw named the same team, even keeping young Garry Brooke as the substitute, while Wolves' star striker Andy Gray missed out due to a hamstring strain suffered at Hillsborough.

Galvin had an early attempt from distance but his shot took a wicked deflection which caused it to slice through the air.

Hibbitt, convicted of diving for the penalty in the first match in the court of public opinion, was booed at every touch.

Steve Perryman lobbed a ball into the box that was seemingly going to be easily dealt with but the Wolves defenders hesitated, looking at each other instead of heading it clear and Garth Crooks raced between them to open the scoring with the 20th goal of his debut season.

George Berry smashed a shot against the underside of the bar and was inches away from equalising for Wolves, and Tottenham somehow survived the ensuing goalmouth scramble, before adding a second goal before half-time when Hoddle robbed the ball after a Wolves throw on Spurs' side of halfway and played it quickly forward. Crooks's pace allowed him to beat the Wolves defenders to the ball. After taking a single touch, Crooks slashed his shot beyond the onrushing Bradshaw.

In the second half, Crooks turned creator. Once again catching Wolves dawdling on the ball, he raced in to snatch the ball and pushed it wide to Villa. The Argentinian drifted inside on his left foot before hammering a left-footed drive for 3-0.

Not since Manchester United's Alex Dawson in 1958 had there been an FA Cup semi-final hat-trick, but in the final moments Crooks seemed certain to break that streak. With the entire Wolves team in the Tottenham half, Hoddle back-heeled to Perryman and the captain pumped the ball long. Crooks, onside and virtually alone, raced on to the ball but instead of taking on the shot, he unselfishly squared for strike partner Archibald.

The Scot produced a remarkable misfire, squibbing his shot well wide of the open goal and the attempt eventually rolled out for a throw.

When the full-time whistle blew, Tottenham fans spilled on to the pitch. A return to Wembley – for the 100th FA Cup Final – had been secured, and on Arsenal's home ground for good measure.

After the match, Crooks admitted that the players had been deflated by the late equaliser in the first tie and credited Burkinshaw with rapidly restoring their morale.

Villa, basking in the afterglow of his sensational goal, was delighted to finally be going to Wembley, calling the Empire Stadium 'the home of football'.

After the match, Perryman admitted that he even felt a little sorry for Wolves because they always seemed to end up losing to Tottenham.

36

Ossie's dream

TWO WEEKS before their date with Manchester City at Wembley, Tottenham's squad were assembled at Portland Studios in Marylebone.

Pop duo Chas & Dave had been convinced by their manager Bob England to write a song for the Spurs players to record and release ahead of the final.

The squad piled into the recording booth to sing the chorus of the song, which would be called 'Ossie's Dream (Spurs Are on Their Way to Wembley)'.

The track was recorded in a single session but not without a minor disagreement. Ossie Ardiles, already reluctant to have the number focused on him alone rather than the team, was required to sing the key line, solo.

The line required the word 'Tottenham' to rhyme with 'man for man'. It would only work if Ardiles sang his club's name the way he had when he had first arrived in England – 'Totting-ham.'

But Ardiles had quickly learned English and was insistent that he sing 'Tottenham' in the typical pronunciation.

After some discussion, Ardiles agreed to sing the line as requested. The great cheer of his team-mates after his line can be heard on the recording.

The Spurs players went on *Top of the Pops* to promote the song, performing alongside 1980s stalwarts Bananarama and Fun Boy Three.

Tony Galvin admits that some alterations were made to the recording, 'It was heavily produced. It sounded a lot worse than that. But it caught the imagination.'

The track was released on the day of the FA Cup Final, 9 May, and eventually reached number five in the UK singles chart.

Steve Perryman had received two tickets to the 1967 FA Cup Final after signing his first Tottenham contract but, 14 years on, he had still not had the chance to play in one. He had played at Wembley for Spurs – and for England schoolboys – but was desperate for the full experience.

Burkinshaw risked the wrath of the FA by leaving Graham Roberts out of Spurs' final league match of the season in order to ensure the rugged midfielder would not be booked and thus suspended for the Wembley final, admitting, 'I probably have broken the rule.'

Spurs were beaten 4-2 by West Bromwich Albion. They hadn't won any of their final six league games and slid down the league to finish tenth, but all focus had long been on Wembley.

Ardiles and Ricky Villa, both named in the starting line-up, became the first non-British players to play in an FA Cup Final since Manchester City goalkeeper Bert Trautmann and his famous broken neck in 1956.

By kick-off the temperature had risen to nearly 19°C. It was a frantic beginning with both sides flying into tackles and the ball whizzing around midfield, but the game eventually settled down. Roberts had the first chance after Perryman bombed a high free kick into the area. The versatile defender rose highest and got his header on target but goalkeeper Joe Corrigan was able to keep it out.

Dave Bennett had a good chance for City midway through the first half, but Roberts got himself in the way. The ensuing corner was a dangerous one but there was no City player there to put it away.

Corrigan then made another vital intervention for City when Galvin, turning his man inside out, had a fine shot turned away for a corner.

Villa looked out of sorts. Three times in the first half he came for a loose ball and missed, allowing City space to attack through, and from the third of those came the opening goal. Seizing the opportunity, City bombed forward and the ball eventually came to Ray Ranson who floated a cross into the box. Scottish midfielder Tommy Hutchison connected powerfully to head his team into the lead.

After 30 minutes Spurs had been the better side but trailed and had to find a way back into the match. It was the first time they'd fallen behind in an FA Cup match in the whole season.

Villa won a header in midfield and flicked the ball into the path of Crooks who raced towards goal, but Corrigan was alert and snuffed out the chance.

Spurs were still on top but City made it to half-time with their lead intact. The expected Tottenham siege hadn't arrived.

In the 68th minute, Villa was caught in possession and City broke quickly. The danger evaporated when Bobby McDonald's cross avoided everyone and went out for a goal kick, but it was Villa's final contribution. The Argentinian was off and Garry Brooke was on in his place.

The image of the tall, bearded Villa dejectedly trudging off and walking back around the cinder track was a powerful one and long-remembered. It was supposed to be a special day, but Villa had been hauled off with his team needing a goal and replaced by a teenager.

It was Tottenham's other Argentinian who changed the game for them. Ardiles robbed back possession in midfield, turned and charged towards goal. He skipped by one challenge and attempted to do the same on the edge of the box but he was fouled and the referee awarded a free kick.

With only ten minutes to go, Spurs needed to make something of this chance and Hoddle stood over it just as he had at Hillsborough. The England midfielder curled his shot towards goal but Corrigan looked to have it covered until Hutchison raced in to attempt to head it clear. Instead, however, City's goalscorer turned the ball into his own net to level the match.

Tottenham had looked out on their feet before the goal, but found their energy renewed and attacked with vigour in the final ten minutes, although neither side could find a winner.

In the first half of extra time Perryman appeared on the right wing. He called for the pass and took it in stride, swinging in a cross to the far post. Galvin was there to head it down but somehow both Brooke and Archibald failed to get a touch that would have almost certainly won it for Tottenham.

With players on both sides barely able to muster a jog, City won a corner late in the second half of extra time. Any goal now would surely be a winner, but Spurs hacked clear. The full time whistle blew less than a minute later.

It was only the second time since FA Cup finals had moved to Wembley in 1923 that there would be a replay. Around 20,000 tickets for the replay were sold to the general public at Wembley the day after the first match. With the proximity of Tottenham, Spurs fans bought the lion's share.

The big question facing Burkinshaw was what to do about Ricky Villa. The Argentinian had had a poor game in the first match, and Perryman told the *Daily Mail* in 2016 that he had advised his manager not to pick him,

'I said, "No chance." I thought he'd turned his back on the team. He felt it was just that Ricky had been so disappointed about his own performance, when it was live on TV back in Argentina. He said, "He's playing."'

Five days after the match, the teams returned to the Empire Stadium with Tottenham unchanged; Villa was given his chance at redemption.

City started well. Chris Hughton cleared off his line in the opening minutes, before Kevin Reeves went down looking for a penalty that never came.

Eight minutes in, Ardiles picked up the ball outside the box on the left wing and drove inside. He rode a challenge and, off balance, fired a shot that fell to Archibald. The Scot only had Corrigan to beat but the City keeper had flown off his line and smothered the shot, but the ball squirmed out of Corrigan's grasp and Villa was there to hammer it home.

After his personal devastation in the first match, Villa sprinted off at top speed in celebration. At first his team-mates couldn't catch him, but they eventually mobbed him to celebrate.

Tottenham's collective joy was short-lived, however. Twenty-year-old Steve MacKenzie levelled the scores just three minutes later with a magnificent volley from the top of the box. The midfielder hit it as sweetly as could be imagined and Milija Aleksic never had a chance of stopping it.

Minutes after the equaliser, Hoddle hit the post with a delicate free kick. Then Aleksic flew out of his area to punch the ball out of the path of Bennett, giving City a dangerous free kick of their own. Fortunately for Spurs, the attempt lacked the quality of Hoddle's and missed the target by some distance.

Corrigan was being peppered with shots. He saved well from Villa and Galvin before half-time, but at the other end, five minutes after the break, Bennett won a penalty after being sandwiched between Miller and Hughton. Reeves converted and Tottenham were chasing the game just as they had been in the first match.

Hoddle seemed likely to score one of the great FA Cup goals when he took the ball in midfield and drove forward, unleashing a wicked shot, but Corrigan was able to push it over the bar.

Then, when City defender Tommy Caton escaped conceding a penalty for handball, it began to seem as though it would not be Tottenham's day.

But in the 70th minute, Villa found Hoddle in space and the number ten lobbed the ball over the advancing back line. Archibald got there first and controlled the ball, but Crooks arrived to stab home the equaliser.

Villa had scored the first goal and been involved in the second, but six minutes later he stepped into immortality.

Roberts won the ball on the edge of Spurs' box and played it to Galvin. The Ireland winger sprinted off, crossed halfway and rolled the ball inside to Villa. Villa had Crooks and Archibald ahead of him, but dribbled towards goal. The City defenders closed in, but Villa floated through two tacklers on the edge of the box. Anticipating Caton's covering tackle, Villa checked back on to his right foot. He was barely seven yards from goal, with Corrigan advancing and six other defenders nearer to him than any team-mate, but still he went on. Just as Corrigan and Caton converged on him, Villa fired his shot into the waiting net to give Spurs the lead.

Eight touches in eight seconds had changed everything.

City still had 15 minutes to play for an equaliser, but Tottenham held on. Archibald, one of the heroes of the campaign, was dribbling towards the corner flag when the final whistle blew. Wembley exploded and Tottenham were FA Cup winners again.

After Perryman had lifted the cup, Ardiles – his dream well and truly having come true – carried it into the dressing room. Then, spotting the players' bath already filled and waiting, he took a long run and leapt in, throwing the trophy in the air as he did. It clanged into the roof of the dressing room, then down into the bath. In the silence that followed,

Hoddle stood over the now thoroughly dented cup, saying, 'What have you done?'

In all the photos taken that evening, and over the following days as the players celebrated their victory, someone always had their hand over the dent.

Forever compared with Bill Nicholson, Keith Burkinshaw delved almost into the realm of cliche after the match, virtually channelling his predecessor when he soberly reflected that Spurs 'perhaps didn't perform as well as we might have done'.

In the afterglow of victory, Hoddle cast his mind back to the draw against Southampton three years earlier on the day they had secured promotion. Ardiles and Villa would certainly not have been at Tottenham if they'd failed to win that game.

Burkinshaw, too, would likely not have survived that failure. Even Hoddle himself, far too bright a light for the Second Division, would probably have moved on.

The romantic Burkinshaw saw in Hoddle the expression of his beliefs, saying, 'For me, Glenn did more work than any of the other players. I've never seen anybody better than [Glenn Hoddle]. He was such a great player.'

It is something of a cliche to suggest that managers are not given the same amount of time as they once were, but it is hard to imagine that Burkinshaw would have survived at Tottenham in the 21st century.

While the relegation cannot be blamed entirely on him, he would certainly have been accused of naivety for persisting with his attacking style. The uncertain nature of the promotion campaign and the two mixed seasons back in the First Division, too, may have seen him moved on.

In the context of FA Cup triumph, it can be more easily seen what Burkinshaw was building towards, and that further successes were to come.

Burkinshaw had faced and overcome the hardship of relegation and the complexity of promotion, the introduction of two big-money duos in Villa and Ardiles, and Crooks and

Archibald. He had held the club together, and built the team they needed to bring the 'glory, glory days' back to White Hart Lane.

Perryman summed up the impact of the Wembley win in 2016, telling the *Daily Mail*, 'It was the day that put Spurs back on the map as a glamour club.'

Epilogue

WHILE NO player's career stretched over this entire period – Pat Jennings's very nearly did – Tottenham Hotspur Football Club had been on an epic journey.

The greatest period the club had ever known – winning the Double and adding British football's first European trophy – slowly drew to a close.

Legends were replaced with mere great players, who in turn were replaced by still lesser players. That long and steady decline manifested in the sad end of Bill Nicholson's time as manager. The club's greatest servant's exit was mishandled, generating bitter feelings that lingered for some time.

The disastrous decision to replace Nicholson with Terry Neill – either unthinkable or thoughtless – saw the last elements of that golden period stripped away.

Then there was a brief window filled with what if moments. What if Tottenham had done as Nicholson recommended and turned to Danny Blanchflower as his successor? What if Neill had successfully signed Johan Cruyff? Indeed, given how goal-shy Spurs were relegated the following season, what if Martin Chivers had convinced the chairman to cancel his transfer after Neill left?

The decision to turn to Keith Burkinshaw in desperation seemed at first bold, then foolish as Tottenham slipped into the Second Division.

The club's willingness to stick with Burkinshaw, as surprising as any of their other decisions in this period, looks inspired in hindsight, as he led them to promotion, and reemergence as one of England's top teams.

After the victory at Wembley, Tottenham would remain a force for the next decade. First under Burkinshaw, then his assistant Peter Shreeves and finally David Pleat, Spurs would continue to win trophies and threaten to add another league title.

They would be transformed under the direction of new owner Irving Scholar, who claimed to have convinced Alex Ferguson to take the Tottenham job as Shreeves's replacement. But Scholar's time in charge ended with the club near bankruptcy, and a takeover by personal computer magnate Alan Sugar.

The 1980s would be Spurs' most successful period since Nicholson, but in the 1990s there was to be another backslide. While the struggling side escaped relegation in the latter part of the decade, there were certainly echoes of the post-Nicholson 1970s decline.

But that decline was far off in 1981. Ahead stood more glory. Another FA Cup was added in 1982. So too a Charity Shield, and a third European trophy would be added in 1984. That UEFA Cup, forever synonymous with Tony Parks's heroics in the penalty shoot-out against Anderlecht, was a poetic final trophy for this group of players for another reason.

After the abrupt end to the Nicholson era, brought about in no small part by the defeat against Feyenoord at De Kuip, Burkinshaw's resurgent Tottenham returned to Rotterdam and won en route to the final in 1984.

Bibliography

Books:

Ardiles, Osvaldo, *Ossie: My Life in Football* (Sidgwick & Jackson, 1983)

Ardiles, Osvaldo, *Ossie's Dream: My Autobiography* (Bantam, 2009)

Bowler, Dave, *Danny Blanchflower: A Biography of a Visionary* (Vista, 1998)

Chivers, Martin, *Big Chiv!: My Goals in Life* (VSP, 2009)

Cloake, Martin, *We are Tottenham: Voices from White Hart Lane* (Edinburgh, 2004)

Davies, Hunter, *The Glory Game* (Edinburgh, 1985)

Duggan, Jim, *The Glory of Spurs: A Fan's Guide to the All-Time Highs and Lows of Tottenham Hotspur* (Crimson, 2012)

Ferris, Ken, *The Double: The Inside Story of Spurs' Triumphant 1960-61 Season* (Mainstream Sport 1999)

Hardin, J., *For the Good of the Game: The Official History of the Professional Footballers' Association* (Robson Books, 1991)

Harris, Harry, *Down Memory Lane* (Green Umbrella, 2009)

Harris, Roxy, and White, Sarah, *Changing Britannia: Life Experience with Britain* (New Beacon Books, 1999)

Hoddle, Glenn, *Playmaker: My Life and the Love of Football* (Harper Collins, 2021)

Hoddle, Glenn, *Spurred to Success* (Macdonald, 1987)

Lowe, Sid, *Fear and Loathing in La Liga: Barcelona vs Real Madrid* (Yellow Jersey Press, 2013)

Mullery, Alan, *Double Bill: The Bill Nicholson Story* (Edinburgh, 2005)

Neill, Terry, *Revelations of a Football Manager* (Sidgwick & Jackson, 1985)

Nicholson, Bill, *Glory Glory: My Life With Spurs* (MacMillan, 1984)

Novick, Jeremy, *Winning Their Spurs: The Tottenham Hotspur Dream Team* (Edinburgh, 1986)

Perryman, Steve, *A Man For All Seasons* (Barker, 1985)

Powley, Adam, *The Boys From White Hart Lane: White Hart Lane in the 80s* (Vision Sports Publishing, 2008)

Roberts, Graham, *When the Going Gets Tough: The Graham Roberts Story* (Edinburgh, 1988)

Sandbrooke, Dominic, *Mad As Hell: The Crisis of the 1970s and the Rise of the Populist Right* (Alfred A. Knopf, 2011)

Scovell, Brian, *Bill Nicholson: Football's Perfectionist* (John Blake, 2011)

Welch, Julie, *The Biography of Tottenham Hotspur* (Vision Sports Publishing, 2012)

Woolnough, Brian, *Glenn Hoddle: The Man and the Manager* (Virgin, 1987)

Websites:
www.britishnewspaperarchive.co.uk
https://archive.org/
https://mehstg.co.uk/wp/
https://11v11.com/

Podcasts:
The Spurs Show
Here Comes Sports Pod

Newspapers:
Aberdeen Press and Journal
Coventry Evening Telegraph
Coventry Standard
Daily Express
Daily Herald
Daily Mail
Daily Mirror
Daily Record
Daily Telegraph
Dundee Courier
Evening Telegraph
Falkirk Herald
Greenock Telegraph
The Guardian
The Herald
The Independent
Irish Independent
Lancashire Evening Post
Leicester Evening Mail
Liverpool Daily Post

Liverpool Echo

Manchester Evening News

Newcastle Evening Chronicle

Newcastle Journal

Nottingham Evening Post

Nottingham Journal

Press and Journal

Reading Evening Post

South Wales Gazette

Sports Argus

Sunday Mirror

The Times

Yorkshire Post